Quick-Sew
DENIM
with no-sew options

Barb Chauncey

Published by

 krause publications
An F&W Publications Company

700 East State Street • Iola, WI 54990-0001
715-445-2214 • 888-457-2873
www.krause.com

To place an order or obtain a free catalog, please call 800-258-0929.

Library of Congress Catalog Number 2003101358

ISBN 0-87349-602-7

Editor: Christine Townsend
Book Designer: Jon Stein and Donna Mummery

Dedication

Dedicated to my mother, Ardath Hinman, who encouraged me to be creative even as a child.

Acknowledgments

There are many people who I wish to thank for their help in making this book possible.

I would like to thank my family for their help and encouragement, especially Stephanie.

Thank you, Jerry, for taking a few pictures. Thanks, Todd, for all those used jeans I don't have to patch now. Thanks to Julie Stephani and Christine Townsend. I appreciate everyone who gave me jeans and helped with photos. Thanks to Doris and her girls, and Maria. Thank you, Lisa, for giving me a boost to get started.

Table of Contents

The History Behind Denim and Jeans

While there is some mystery—even controversy—about the true origin of denim fabric, we know it was being produced in both France and England by the end of the seventeenth century. But where did it originate?

There was a town in France named Nîmes where a serge fabric, serge de Nîmes, was made from silk and wool. Fabrics often were named for their geographic place of origin, and since the word "denim" sounds like it could be a derivation of the French town "de Nîmes," it seems logical to assume that denim came from this French town. What we call denim today, though, isn't made from silk or wool, it's made from cotton.

We also know that there was a cotton fabric called "jean" that was first made in Genoa, Italy. Like serge de Nîmes, jean was also a twill weave. But denim, the stronger and more expensive cloth, was made from one colored thread and one white thread; jean, however, was made from two threads of the same color. To complicate matters more, mills throughout Europe made jean and denim, capitalizing on the romance associated with their "foreign" names. Because there aren't official records regarding where these mills received the fabrics they imitated, their real origins remain murky.

In the eighteenth century, American mills began to produce both denim and jean. The first printed reference to "denim" appeared well over 200 years ago, in a Rhode Island newspaper dated 1769. Denim and jean fabrics were much in demand in America. But the denim cloth was comfortable, durable, and easily laundered. It was used mainly as material to make trousers for those who performed manual labor, from coal miners to ranchers. Jean, although it was strong, was considered more "formal," and so was used to make more tailored trousers.

In the early days of America, jeans were referred to as "waist overalls." When Levi Strauss and Jacob Davis invented their copper-riveted version, they made them from blue and brown denim; hence, denim overalls. It was not until after World War II that they were actually referred to as "jeans"—and it seems as though the name was just what Americans *chose* to call them. It was around 1970 that jeans were widely accepted for all occupations—not just the working or labor classes. We love the stuff!

What are *you* wearing? I'm in jeans.

Selecting Denim and Techniques for Denim Crafting

Choose the Right Pair of Jeans

Selecting the right pair of jeans to work with is an important first step in creating any project. When collecting old jeans, pay attention to whether they are light or dark, slim or wide, plain or embellished. It is often helpful to select jeans with a particular project in mind in order to get the perfect pair—or pairs.

If you do not have enough old denim lying around the house, check out thrift shops or garage sales. Thrift shops sometimes sort out jeans that are too shabby to sell. You may be able to obtain these free of charge. The change of seasons usually brings a new pile of discarded jeans at garage sales. Look for jeans with unusual pockets, buttons, or loops.

At first glance, you might think a pair of jeans is useless, as many discarded jeans have faded knees or worn hems. I have found that the backside of jeans often have more uniform color and fewer stains. And, don't overlook a great waistband or perfectly useable pockets on an otherwise worn pair of jeans.

Denim comes in many shades of blue ... some lighter, some darker.

Select the Right Weight

Select the weight of denim to suit the project. In general, if the finished product needs to stand by itself, use heavier or stiffer denim. Gift bags are easier to make from stiffer denim. If the project has many folds or is very small, use lighter weight or softer denim. Use thinner denim for projects that require edges to be folded around mat board or notebooks.

Select the Right Color

Denim comes in many shades of blue … some lighter, some darker. This contrast is especially important in woven projects, such as some of the pillows. A checkerboard effect can be achieved by alternating light and dark strips.

Utilize Unique Features

Unusual yokes or pockets can make a pillow top.

Striped bib overalls usually have many unique pockets and buttons, and the striped denim fabric adds a special look. The suspenders make great handles on purses or other bags. The suspender top and pockets from bib overalls would make an interesting pillow top. Another idea is to add darker fabric behind the suspenders for a splash of color and contrast.

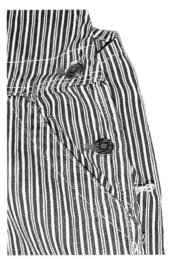

Storage

Store denim pieces as flat as possible, whether hung from hangers or folded. This keeps the denim from wrinkling. Wrinkles can be difficult to press out; spray them with a little water and then press with a steam iron.

You may be tempted to cut the jeans into large pieces to store them, but it is best to wait to do any cutting until you have selected the project for which you'll use them. That way, you'll be sure to have the right size fabric for the right project and, since some denims can fray when cut, you'll have less of a mess!

Utilize unique features.

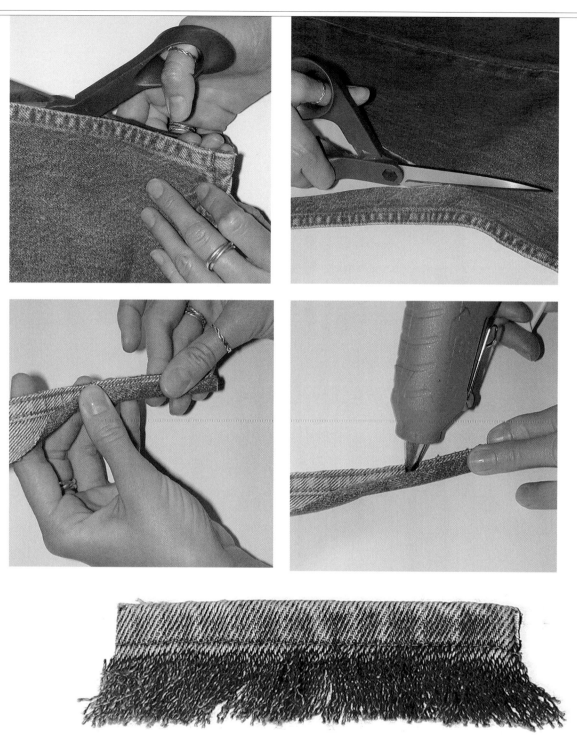

The technique of braid making

Finishing Edges

Denim does not ravel easily on raw edges, but folding the raw edges under gives a more finished look. The edge of a piece of denim can be fringed by pulling out the threads that go crosswise to the grain of the fabric. The process takes time, but may give the desired effect. If the white threads are pulled out, blue fringe results. Pulling these threads is harder and takes more time. A seam can be used to stop the fraying.

If the thinner blue threads are pulled, a heavier white fringe appears along the edge of the fabric. If threads are pulled on both sides of a strip of fabric, it looks like denim ribbon with a fringed edge.

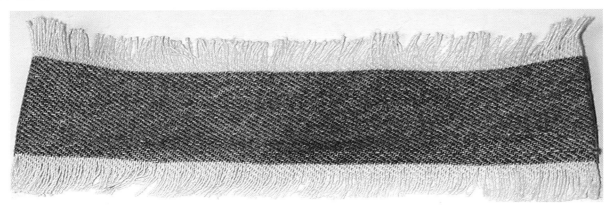

Techniques

Making a Strap from a Double-Stitched Seam

To make a strap or decorative strip with the classic double-stitched denim seams, cut very close to the seam on the overlapped edge. Cut about ³⁄₄" from the double-stitching on the other side. Fold the raw edge under twice to hide the raw edge, and glue in place.

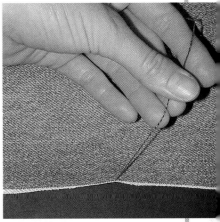

Making Denim Braid

Cut three strips of double-stitched seams, and finish the back as described on page 8. Braid the three strands; secure the ends with clear hot glue. This trim is great for the front of a larger notebook or album, across the top of a purse or bag, or on a plain, denim pillow top. If the braid is used as a handle, a piece of wire can be placed on the back of the seam and covered by the overlapped fabric when finishing the edge of each strand. It may only be necessary to include wire in one of the strands to make it stiff enough to hold its shape. Strands that are 30" long result in a braid that is 24" long.

Keep the braid loose enough so that it will lay flat. Braiding too tightly may result in a curved braid that will be difficult to flatten.

Making a Strip for Weaving

To straighten the edge of denim, pull a thread until it goes all along the edge. Trim excess fringe and the edge will be straight with the grain of the fabric. Cut strips of denim the width you want for the finished weaving plus ³⁄₈" on each side to turn under so raw edges don't show. Gluing the edges back is fast, but results in a stiffer finished product. If you are making a pillow to actually lie on, the glue will make it feel too hard and stiff. It may also be more economical to sew the edges when turning the raw edge to the back. A decorative stitch can be used even on just a few of the strips for a special look.

The length of the strips will be determined by the project. Remember, strips can be woven into a piece of cloth, then that piece can be cut on the diagonal for a classy effect.

If lengthwise strips are dark and crosswise strips are lighter, a checkerboard effect will result. If you want a more random look, even-weave the strips first before tacking any in place with glue—then stand back and look at the weaving from a distance, as it will look a little different than it does up close.

Pockets

To remove a pocket from a pair of jeans, cut very close to the pocket on all edges except the top. Leave enough fabric to turn under for a finished look or to attach to another piece. Be sure to clip the top corners of the fabric above the pocket before turning it under. This will eliminate bulk at the corners.

Remember to cut out those little "inside pockets" that can be found on the right front side of some jeans. These little pockets are especially cute and just the right size for a few pennies or other small items. Some of the edges of these inside pockets are not hemmed. These edges can be folded under or covered by another piece of fabric or trim, so do not discard the inside pockets just because they have unfinished edges.

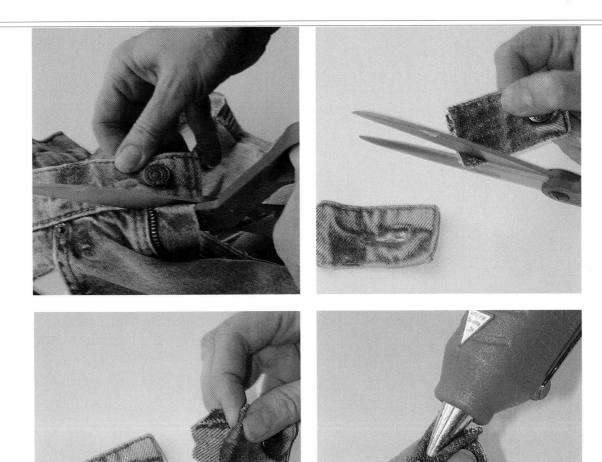

Waistbands

Cut close to the lower edge of the waist-band to remove it from the jeans. To remove the waistband from the rest of the jeans, you will need to cut the lower edge of the belt loops from the body of the jeans. Leave the belt loops attached to the waistband itself. The lower edge of the belt loops can be glued onto the project as they were sewn onto the jeans.

For some projects, the waistband needs to be opened up along the bottom edge to allow it to be attached to the rest of the project. It usually can be ripped open with a seam ripper. Excess fabric inside the band may also be trimmed away to eliminate bulk when adding it to the project.

Waistband snaps or buttons can be used as closures by cutting a few inches beyond the snap or buttonhole. Rip the bottom stitching open about an inch, and cut away excess fabric. Clip corners. Tuck the raw edges inside the waistband. Glue or stitch the opening closed. It may be easier to glue this edge if the button or snap would get in the way of the sewing machine needle, or if the piece is too bulky.

Projects:
Around the House

Roll Pillow

Who would guess that this pillow was once a pant leg? The ends simply tie closed, but the weaving creates a unique look. Hunt for jeans with a long and very straight leg …
and be prepared to sew on lots of bias tape!

Materials:

- 2 denim pant legs, at least 28" long
- 6 strips of striped denim from bib overalls, 19" x 1½"
- 9 yd. red bias tape
- Fiberfill or quilt batting

Supplies:

- Measuring tape or stick
- Sewing machine
- Glue gun and clear glue
- Scissors
- Pins

Instructions

1. Cut the pant leg just below the pocket, and cut off the bottom hem. The resulting piece should be at least 28" long. Cut from the top of the leg along the double-stitched seam to a point where the leg straightens out. Cut away excess fabric to make the seam straight.

2. Measure 10" from the top end and mark with a pin. Stitch (or glue) the seam closed below this point. Cut open the other seam 10" from the top.

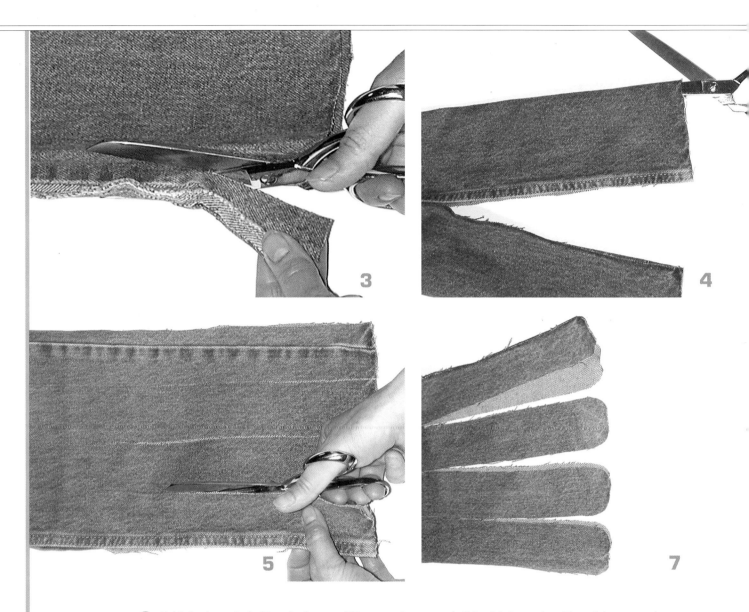

3 Fold the jeans in half so the hem end lies over the top end. Trim fabric on the sides of the top end to match the hem end in width. Unfold the fabric. Measure 10" from the hem end and cut along the double-stitched seam. Make sure the leg is lying flat, and cut up 10" on the opposite side. *Note: This may not be on the seam line when the leg is flat.*

4 Now, fold the front half of the hem end in half to find the center, and cut up to the 10" line. Fold each of those pieces in half, and cut again to the 10" line. This makes four equal strips of fabric.

5 Lay the leg flat again and use these strips to show where to cut strips in the back of the leg.

6 Fold the leg in half, end-to-end, and use one set of the strips to show where to cut the strips at the top end.

7 Cut off the corners of each strip to a rounded shape. Rip the double-stitched seam open to the 10" line, and remove excess fabric along the edge of that strip.

8 Sew bias tape along the edges of the slits, starting at one side and continuing around, strip after strip, until you are back to where you started.

9 To join two pieces of bias tape: Unfold strips, lay at right angles, pin, and stitch diagonally from right to left side.

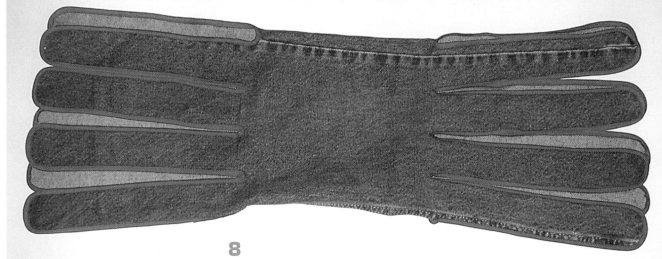

8

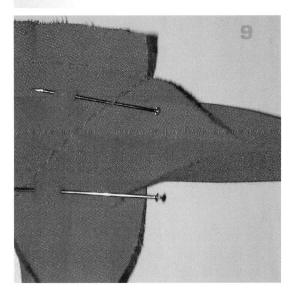

9

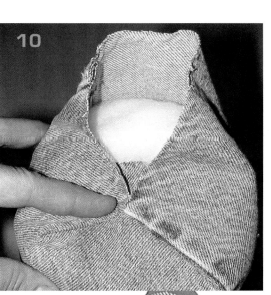

10

10 To fill the pillow: Make a sleeve from the other leg, straightening as in step 1. Stuff, with fiberfill or a rolled piece of quilt batting, to within 2½" of the end. Fold the ends in and glue in place.

11 Insert this form into the pillow. Hem edges of striped denim by turning the raw edges under ¼" and stitching (or gluing). Weave these strips into the ends of the pillow, hiding the ends and gluing to secure. Glue each tab of the final strip.

12 To finish the ends, tie the opposite tabs together until all are tied. Secure with a little glue in the knot so it will not come untied.

12

Woven Wall Hanging

Weave large strips of denim into this versatile wall hanging. You can vary its size through the length and number of strips you weave. The strips offer a fun way to display wallet-size photos since they fit in the woven spaces. The whole wall hanging could be mounted on cork or thick foam core so that it would be more like a covered bulletin board.

I chose a butterfly-and-rainbow-colors theme for this wall hanging. The butterflies are made with colored hot glue—a really fun craft medium.

Instructions

1 Prepare all denim strips by folding back the long edge of the denim ⅜", and gluing it down. Lay the long strips side by side, and begin weaving shorter strips through them. Secure the ends with hot glue, or tack with pins until you are finished. Secure edges with glue.

2 When cutting double-stitched seams to put around the edge of the weaving, cut 1½" from the seam on one side. Begin by attaching the side pieces. Glue the double-stitched seam over the edge of the denim weaving. Fold the raw edge under ¼", and tack with glue or stitching. Then fold the denim

Materials:

- 9 strips denim, 3¼" x 34½"
- 12 strips denim, 3¼" x 25"
- 2 double-stitched seams, 35½" long
- Double-stitched seam, 26" long
- Waistband, 25½" long
- Midwest basswood, ³⁄₁₆" x 2" x 24"
- 2 picture hangers
- Trim of your choice, 52"
- Mirror, 2" x 3"
- 18mm round faceted stones, multi-colors (The Beadery)
- 12 mirror tiles, 1" square
- 22 gauge wire in Bare Copper, Kelly Green, Light Brown, Powder Blue

Supplies:

- Scissors
- Ruler
- Glue gun and clear glue
- Colored hot glue: yellow, purple, blue metallic, orange, green, white
- Pins
- Non-stick working surface
- Wire cutters
- Hammer
- Heat gun
- Needle-nose pliers

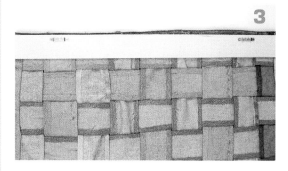

3

6

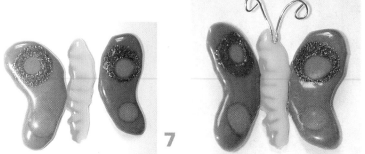

7

beside the double-stitched seam to the back, and glue it to the back of the weaving. The raw ends on the top will be covered by other pieces, so they do not need to be finished. The raw ends on the bottom piece need to be turned under to give them a finished look.

3 Cut the waistband for the top edge ¾" longer than the weaving so you can open the cut end and tuck the raw edges to the inside. Then glue the waistband over the top edge of the weaving. Glue the loose ends of the belt loops down to the weaving.

4 Use the hammer and small nails to attach the picture hangers to the top edge of the piece of basswood—about 3" from each end. Quickly spread a large amount of hot glue along the edges of the backside of the basswood and place it along the top edge (backside) of the wall hanging.

5 Cut the trim to fit across the top and bottom of the wall hanging, adding enough to turn under to finish the edges. Tack in place with clear hot glue.

6 Arrange the mirror tiles and attach with hot glue. Remember that the edges can be sharp, so handle the mirror pieces carefully.

7 To make the hot glue butterflies: Prepare colored dots for wings by squeezing some glue onto the non-stick surface and cool it in a refrigerator for a few minutes. Then use a paper punch to punch out dots. A slice can be cut from the ends of two colored glue sticks of contrasting color. Punch holes in the center of each, and put the small circle back into the slice of the opposite color. Use the heat gun to melt it a little on the non-stick surface. Cool. Then put it onto a hot wing shape. This makes a dot, like the top one, on the purple wing.

8 To make the wings: Squeeze glue into matching wing shapes on a non-stick surface. While the glue is hot, place dots onto the wing shapes. If the glue is too cool to allow them to melt, carefully heat the glue with a heat gun—too much blowing will distort the shape of the glue. Make the body shape by adding yellow glue after green glue in the gun. When both colors start to mix, make a body shape. Make an antenna by cutting a piece of wire 2¼" long. Use needle-nose pliers to curl the ends and bend the wire in the center. Either add the antenna to a heated body, or use clear glue to add it. Wings can be added in the same way.

9 This butterfly was made by squeezing out wing shapes of blue metallic glue and putting a yellow dot into them. When the glue gun needs another stick, put a white stick in and squeeze out enough glue so white and blue are coming out mixed. Now, squeeze dots of the mixed glue around the edge of the blue metallic. Cool. Use a ⅛" punch to make holes around the edge. The body for the butterfly was made with yellow glue that had blue metallic mixed into it. Join the body parts with a little clear glue. You can hold the wings up a little so it looks like the butterfly is flying.

Tips: If the wing shapes you have made are not quite the right shape, you can trim them with scissors. If, when you do trim them, the edges show scissor marks, heat the edges a little with the heat gun. Always use a non-stick surface when heating the glue. Body shapes also can be cut from a flat piece of glue.

10 Place butterflies onto the wall hanging on a shade of denim that allows them to show up well. Glue faceted stones near butterflies for more sparkle.

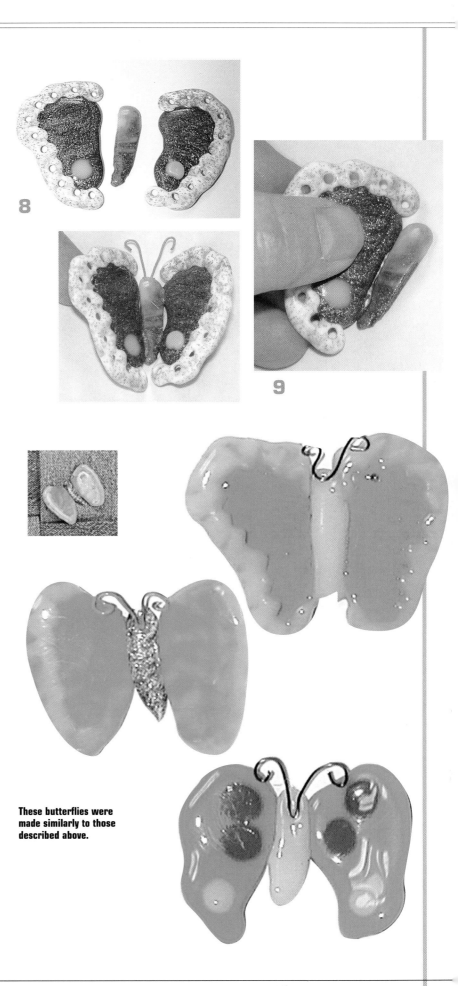

These butterflies were made similarly to those described above.

Lined Pocket Pouch

This version of the pocket pouch has no handle, but instead features a larger lined center area with the pockets around the outside. The square plastic container that forms the base should be somewhat smaller than the pockets, so that the pockets can gap open to hold more things. Be sure to select pockets that are the same length along the side.

Materials:

- 2 pairs of denim pockets
- Fabric, 24" x 10"
- Square plastic container
- Cardboard to fit bottom of plastic container

Supplies:

- Scissors
- Sewing machine
- Thread
- Glue gun and clear glue
- Colored hot glue: orange, yellow
- Clear acrylic sheet
- 1/8" paper punch

Instructions

1 Cut out pockets and glue the top edges back. Use clear hot glue to join the pockets along the sides to form a circle of pockets.

2 To make the lining: Measure around the inside of the pocket circle, and add 1" for length of the lining fabric. Measure the depth of the pockets, and add 1" for width of the lining fabric. Cut out the lining using these measurements. Hem the top edge and one end by turning under ¼" and stitching.

3 Glue the lining to inside the edge of the pocket, starting with the unhemmed end of the fabric at one corner.

4 Continue gluing all around and overlap the hemmed end of the lining over the unhemmed end. Allow the glue to cool thoroughly.

5 Be sure the square plastic container is at least ½" smaller along each side than the pockets. If the container is the same size as the pockets, they would be held tightly against the sides of the container and would not be able to hold anything very thick. The smaller container allows them to gap open and hold more. Trim the cardboard to fit loosely inside the bottom of the container. (It

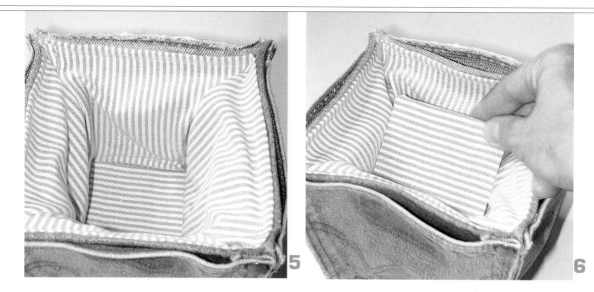

should be about $\frac{1}{8}$" smaller on each side than the bottom of the container to allow for the lining fabric.) Place the container between pockets and lining by pulling the pockets down over the container. Smooth the lining fabric into the bottom of the container, pleating the excess fabric at the corners.

6   Cut the fabric on each side $\frac{1}{2}$" larger than the cardboard. Trim the corners, and glue the fabric to the back of the cardboard at the corners first, then along each side. Put hot glue on the back of the cardboard up to $\frac{1}{2}$" of the edge. Push the cardboard down into the bottom of the plastic container. This will hold the lining fabric in place.

7   Decorate the outside of the pockets with colored hot glue. Apply orange glue in a rectangular shape on a scrap of denim. Let cool. Make letters to spell "stamps," "pens," etc., on a clear acrylic sheet (or other non-stick surface) so you can try again if a letter is the wrong size or otherwise misshapen. If a letter, such as "o", needs a hole, allow the letter to cool and then punch the hole with a $\frac{1}{8}$" paper punch. Allow the letters to cool. Place them inside the rectangle with a little hot glue.

Mini Pocket Pouch

This mini pocket pouch holds tiny necessities, and is just so cute! It is made from the "inside pockets" usually found inside the right hand pocket of jeans. It could also be made from children's jeans pockets. It is so small that it stands without a wooden base.

Materials:

- 4 small denim pockets
- Trim to go around pockets, 1 yd.
- 6" double-stitched seam

Supplies:

- Scissors
- Glue gun and clear glue

Instructions

1. Cut around the pockets. Hem or glue the bottom edge under if the pocket is not finished along the bottom.

2. Stitch or glue the trim all the way around two pockets and along the bottom edge of the other two pockets. Then glue the pockets to each other along the sides to form a circle of pockets.

3. Make a 6" piece of double-stitch seam into a handle by folding it in half and gluing the ends together. Pinch the insides of the pockets next to each other together and glue almost to the center. Glue the handle into the middle.

Twig 'n Leather Pocket Pouch

Sporting twigs and leather,   *this pocket pouch has a rustic, lodge look.*

Materials:

- 2 pairs of denim pockets
- Leather Factory Velvet Suede Trim Piece, gold
- Fiebing's Leathercraft Cement
- Twig, $\frac{3}{8}$" x $13\frac{1}{2}$"
- Pine board, 1" x 5" x 5"
- 18 gauge wire, 40"

Supplies:

- Scissors
- Glue gun, clear hot glue
- Band saw or jig saw
- Sander or sandpaper
- Drill with $\frac{3}{8}$" bit
- Wood glue
- Needle-nose pliers

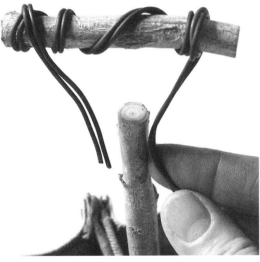

Instructions

1. Follow steps 1 and 2 from the directions on page 30.

2 Glue fabric at the top of pockets to the back, then glue pockets together, side-by-side, to form a circle of pockets. Pinch together the inside fabric of two adjacent pockets to the center of the pockets, and glue along the top edge. Repeat with the other sets of pockets, making sure to leave a hole in the center for the twig to go through.

3 Cut a piece of twig 3" for top of handle. Glue the rest of the twig into the hole in the wooden base. Push the pockets down over the twig, and glue the pockets to the twig in the center, and to the base along the beveled edge of the base.

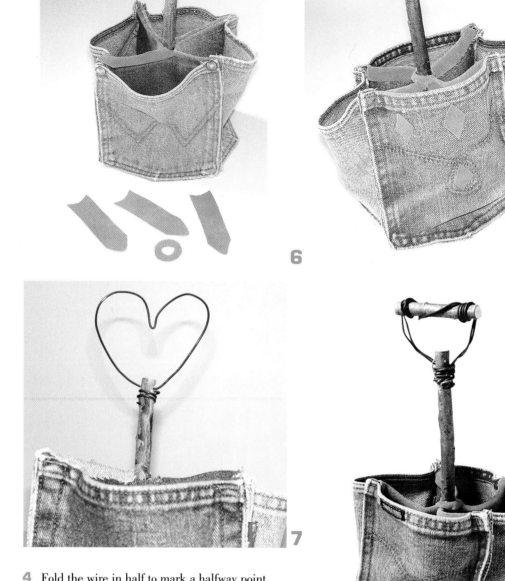

4 Fold the wire in half to mark a halfway point. Lay one cut end next to the twig and bend the wire out to form the side of the handle.

5 Next, wrap it closely three times around the 3" twig. Now, wrap loosely to the other end of the 3" twig, and wrap around that end three times closely. Bend the wire down to form the opposite side of the handle. Wrap the remaining wire around the dowel tightly, covering the starting end of the wire. use a needle-nose pliers to crimp down wire end.

6 Cut pieces of the velvet suede trim 1" wide, and the length (from center to edge) of each pocket. Trim one end of each piece to a rounded point and curve the other end slightly to fit the center post. Cut a disc to fit around the center post, covering the other ends of the suede. Use Leathercraft Cement to glue the suede to the pocket fabric. Extra suede can be made into other shapes and glued to the outside of the pockets for added interest.

7 A wire heart top can be made by drilling a hole crosswise through the twig about ½" from the top of the twig. Cut a piece of wire 24" long. Pull about 12" of the wire through the hole, and form it into a heart shape. Push the end of the wire back into the hole. Then wrap the remaining wire around and around the twig. Grasp the end with the needle-nose wire pliers and push it into the twig or flatten it to the twig to prevent things from catching on it.

Star Topper Pocket Pouch

This unique use of pockets makes a real conversation piece as well as a great organizer for whichever room you choose … colors and toppers can be changed to fit your décor. Or, top the pockets with an apple, and you've got the perfect gift for a favorite teacher.

Be sure to select four pockets that are similar in size—especially in height. Place matching pockets opposite each other.

Materials:

- 2 pairs of denim pockets
- 2½ yd. Wrights Lip Cord Trim
- Dowel, ³/₈" x 12"
- Pine board, 1" x 6" x 7"
- Delta Ceramcoat acrylic paint, Custard and Coastline Blue
- Surebonder® yellow colored hot glue
- 2" wooden star shape, Woodworks Limited

Supplies:

- Glue gun and clear glue
- Band saw or jig saw
- Sander or sandpaper
- Drill with ³/₈" bit
- Paintbrush
- Plastic pallet
- Water
- Wood glue

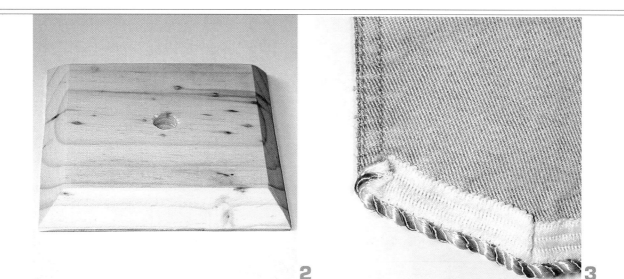

2

3

4

Glue Option

Fold the pocket ends toward the center, and glue the trim to the back of the pocket bottom. Repeat on a second matching pocket. Fold the fabric at the top of the pocket back and glue. Place two pockets back-to-back, with trim between. Glue pockets together ½" from the center of the pocket to make the center hole when all of the pockets have been joined. Clip the lip of the trim at the corner and continue gluing down the pocket sides. At the bottom corner, clip the lip of the trim and glue the trim to bottom edge of one of the pockets. Add another pocket back-to-back, and glue up the side. Clip the corner of the lip and glue to center. Leave an extra 1" of trim at center end so the raw edge can be tucked inside the center hole. Repeat until all of the pockets have been joined.

Instructions

1 Cut out the pockets close to the edge with ½" fabric above pocket (see General Directions on page 10); pockets must be the same size along their sides.

2 Measure across the bottom edge of one of each pair of pockets, and cut the pine board into a rectangle ¼" smaller (both length and width) than the width of the pocket. Drill a ⅜" hole in the center of the board for the dowel. Sand the board smooth. Sand the corners to a beveled shape.

3 Measure a piece of trim to fit along the bottom of one pocket, and add 1". Trim ½" of the lip of the trim from each end. Fold the ends toward the center, and stitch the trim to the back of the bottom of the pocket. Repeat on a second matching pocket. Fold the fabric at the top of the pocket back, and stitch or pin-baste. Place two pockets back-to-back with trim between. Begin stitching them together ½" from the center of the pockets—this will make a center hole when all of the pockets are joined. Clip the lip of the trim at the corner, and continue stitching down the side of the pocket. At the bottom corner, clip the lip of the trim and stitch to the bottom edge of one of the pockets.

4 Add another pocket back-to-back, and stitch up the side. Clip the corner of the lip and stitch to the center. Leave an extra 1" of trim at the center end so the raw edge can be tucked inside the center hole. Repeat this process until all the pockets have been joined.

5 Paint the dowel with Custard Ceramcoat, and the star with Coastline Blue. Allow them to dry. Apply wood glue to the end of the dowel, and place in the hole in the center of the wood base. Slip the pockets over the dowel through the hole in the center of the pockets, and pull down over the wooden base. Attach the pockets to the base with hot glue along the beveled edge of the base. Apply colored hot glue to outline the star. When the glue is set, use wood glue to attach the star to the top of the dowel.

Pocket Tree

*What a fun way to organize your collection of necessary things!
This pocket tree can be decorated to fit your style and needs.
It can even serve as an Advent Calendar at Christmas time—
fill it with little surprises for someone special.*

Materials:
- 25 pockets of various sizes and shades
- Kreative Kanvas, 24" x 25"

Supplies:
- Scissors
- Glue gun and clear glue

Instructions

1. Cut out pockets. Fold top edge of the fabric back and glue down. Arrange the pockets into tree shape on the Kreative Kanvas. Squeeze the pockets' sides in a little so they will open farther to put things in. If they are glued very flat, they will only hold thin things. Pin or glue the pockets together, so they will remain in place when you remove them from the backing. On the Kreative Kanvas, trace around the outside edge of the pockets. Remove the pockets from the canvas.

2. Use scissors to cut the edge of the Kreative Kanvas slightly smaller than pockets. Place pockets back onto the canvas. Glue pockets to the backing, beginning with pockets that are underneath other pockets, and generally working from bottom to top.

3. Add trim with clear hot glue.

Woven Corner Pillow

The corners of this pillow can be made using bias tape or orange hot glue. The glue option is more challenging. If you choose to glue, you must also glue the blue tape all around the edge, because trying to stitch through glue will gum up your sewing machine or needle. If orange isn't for you, choose another color with high contrast for a dramatic effect.

Materials:

- 2 denim pant legs
- 4 light colored denim strips 1⁵/₈" x 31"
- 14" Fairfield Soft Touch pillow insert
- 4 yd. orange bias tape OR 4 orange glue sticks
- 1²/₃ yd. blue extra-wide bias tape

Supplies:

- Scissors
- Quilter's square
- Ruler
- Thread
- Sewing machine OR glue gun and clear glue
- Pins

1

2

3

4

Finishing Options:

Glue Option

Join back and front of pillow, wrong sides together, with glue along three sides. Glue one side of the blue wide-bias tape to the front edge of the pillow and then to the back edge all around three sides. Place the pillow insert into the pillow. Glue the fourth side closed. Continue gluing tape to the fourth side. Fold the end of the tape under ¼", and glue over the first end to cover the raw end.

Sewing Option

Pin back and front of pillow, wrong sides together, and fold the tape over both front and back of the pillow. Stitch the tape around three sides of the pillow, joining front and back. Place the pillow insert inside the pillow. Stitch the remaining side closed with bias tape. Overlap ends, folding tape under ¼" to hide raw end.

Instructions

1 Cut pant legs along the double-stitched seam. Use the quilter's square to mark a line on the wrong side of the denim pant leg at a 90 degree angle to the seam at the larger end of the fabric. This makes the seam go down the center of the pillow, instead of at a crooked angle.

2 Draw lines to form a 15" square. Make two identical pieces—one for the front and one for the back of the pillow.

Step 3 Sew Option:

Trace pattern lines onto the back of one denim square, and cut down each line. Stitch the orange bias tape to line each slit.

Step 3 Glue Option:

Trace lines on front of denim and apply colored glue to either side of the line, leaving a ⅛" space between glue lines. Stop adding glue ³⁄₁₆" from the edges. Allow the glue to cool. Cut lines to open slits.

4 Prepare weaving strips by stitching (or gluing) the raw edges under ¼". Weave the strips into the corners, cutting at angles to match the side of the pillow. Stitch around the pillow ¼" from the edge to secure woven strips.

Pocket Heart

Pockets are great for holding all those little things, and this heart has a place for just about everything. Necklaces can hang from the buttons on the sides. The belt loops can hold sunglasses or scissors. Since it is made on foam core, you can even use the center as a miniature bulletin board. It goes together quickly, and would make a great gift for a friend.

Materials:

- 8 pockets
- Fabric for center, 12" x 12" (depending on pockets sizes)
- 2 button tabs
- 2 belt loops
- Double-stitched seam for hanger, 8"
- Foam core, 24" x 24"
- Trim, 48"

Supplies:

- Scissors
- Pins
- Ruler
- Craft knife
- Glue gun and clear glue

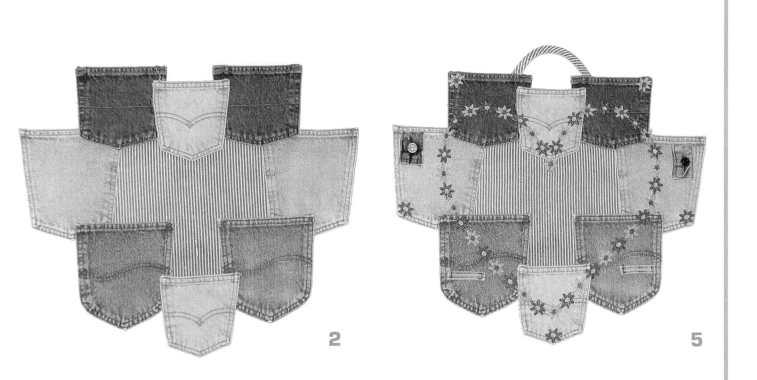

2   5

Instructions

1 Cut out pockets. Fold the top edge of the fabric back and glue down. Place the fabric in the center of the foam core. Arrange the pockets into a heart shape on the foam core. Squeeze pockets a little side-to-side so they will open enough for thicker things. If they are glued very flat, they will only hold thin things. Tack or pin the pockets to each other, so they will stay connected when you move them off the foam core. On the foam core, trace around outside edge of pockets. Remove the pockets from the foam core.

2 Using a ruler and craft knife, cut the edge of foam core slightly smaller than the pockets. Place the fabric and pockets back onto the foam core. Fold the pockets in half, and begin gluing the fabric to foam core, working from the center to the edge, making sure all edges will line up when finished. When the first half is glued, work from the center to the other edge, gluing fabric and pockets down.

3 Pin the trim in a heart-shape over the pockets. If you need a pattern, use a large sheet of paper folded in half and draw, then cut a heart shape. Use hot glue to hold the trim in place, removing pins as you glue. Other individual pieces of trim can be glued to the corners of some of the pockets.

4 Cut the button end from the waistband, so when $\frac{1}{4}$" is folded inside on the cut end, the button will be in the center of the piece. Trim corners from cut end. Remove excess seam allowance, tuck ends inside, and glue closed. Glue onto side pockets so a necklace or other object can hang down from the button.

5 Prepare an 8" strip of double-stitched seam as described in the General Directions, page 9. Glue the ends inside the corner of the top pockets to make a hanger.

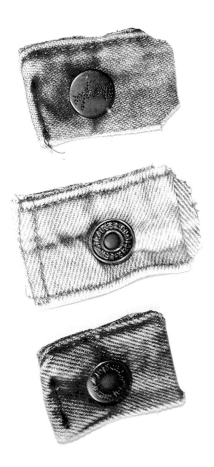

A new denim pillow will brighten up almost any sofa or chair, bed or corner. It makes a great handmade gift. If you use contrasting shades of denim, you will get a polished checkerboard effect. However, if the strips are placed randomly, the pillow will have a more casual look. Try weaving, then stand back and look from a distance to get the real effect of your design. Stitching the edges of the strips takes more time, but yields a softer pillow.

Materials:

GLUE OPTION FOR 18" PILLOW

- 9 strips dark denim, 2³/₄" x 19"
- 9 strips light denim, 2³/₄" x 19"
- Denim for pillow back 19" x 19"
- Pillow insert, 18" x 18"
- 2 yd. Wright's covered cording, lt. blue
- Surebonder® Fabric Stik™, 3 or 4 sticks
- Surebonder glue gun
- Therm O Web Heat'n Bond R Ultra Hold
- Iron on adhesive, 17" x 17"

SEWING OPTION FOR 16" PILLOW

- 7 strips dark denim, 3" x 17"
- 7 strips light denim, 3" x 17"
- Denim for pillow back 17" x 17"
- Pillow insert, 16" x 16"
- 68" Wright's small lip cord, medium blue
- Hot pink thread
- 3 yd. Wright's pink flowered trim
- Lightweight blue cotton fabric, 17" x 17"

Supplies:

- Scissors
- Tape measure
- Iron
- Heavy needle
- Pins
- Glue gun and clear glue OR sewing machine

Gluing everything is possible and is better for a strictly decorative pillow since it makes the pillow stiffer to the touch. It is best to choose all glue or all stitching, since it is difficult to stitch around the edge of the pillow if the strips are glued—it may gum up the needle or sewing machine parts.

Instructions

1 Cut strips of denim. Fold edge under ⅜" and stitch or glue. Sew the trim on the edges of two light colored strips and two dark strips.

2 Lay the dark strips next to each other. Weave in the light strips.

Step 3 Sew Option:

Around the outside edge of pillow, top stitch again parts that have a denim strip passing under them. This keeps them from "cracking open" when the pillow is stuffed. Pin cording in place around the edge with the raw edge of the cording along the raw edges of the denim. Start the cording on a matching (darker) block of the denim a little past the corner, overlapping ends as in photo. Stitch close to the cording using a zipper foot.

Step 3 Glue Option:

Glue strip ends. Dot glue under all light squares to add stability. Glue the cording raw edge to raw edge, in place all around the pillow. Allow to cool completely.

4 To make the pillow back, cut open the back of jeans to the yoke to straighten the seam.

5 Fold the top seam allowance back in a straight line; lay it over other the side of the jeans leg and stitch or glue down.

6 Pin, right sides together, the pillow front and back. Cut around the pillow top, making sure it is completely flat so pillow back will be large enough.

7 For a plain pillow back, remove the seams from two pant legs that are at least 9" wide at their narrowest point. Straighten the edges by marking and cutting in a straight line. Stitch or glue to join pieces. Cut back as in step 5.

Finishing Options:

Sew Option

Lay pillow top and back right sides together, and stitch around three sides of the pillow following the cording stitch line. Clip the fabric from the corners. Turn right side out. Push pillow insert into pillow. Hand stitch pillow closed.

Glue Option

Turn edge of pillow front under and tack with glue. When cooled, turn edge of pillow back under and glue to pillow front on three sides. Place pillow insert inside and glue opening closed.

Handbags and Totes

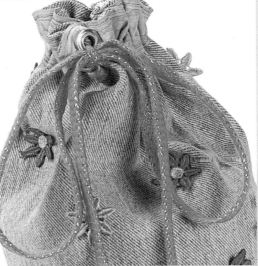

Grampa's Bibs Barrel Bag

The shape for these bags comes from the plastic containers that are in the bottom of each bag. A gallon size orange juice container was cut for the larger bag so it has more of a rectangular shape. The strap buttons on and off, so it is detachable. Weaving red trim through a series of belt loops makes the checkerboard effect on the next bag. You can use a favorite pocket for the flap on the bag. The next variation is a simple bag that can be dressed up with your choice of trim.

Materials:

- [ ] 18½" lower leg of bib overalls
- [ ] 4¾" x 21" strip of overall fabric for strap
- [ ] Front and side pockets from overalls
- [ ] 2 buttons from side of overalls
- [ ] Rectangular plastic gallon container
- [ ] 48" heavy cord
- [ ] 2¼" grommets
- [ ] Red hot glue or red bias cording
- [ ] Red thread

Supplies:

- [ ] Scissors
- [ ] Ruler
- [ ] Pins
- [ ] Sewing machine
- [ ] Glue gun and clear glue
- [ ] Grommet kit
- [ ] Hammer
- [ ] Acrylic board

Instructions

1   Cut around gallon container 4" from bottom edge. Check to see how the cut container fits inside the overall leg. If the leg is too large, stitch a seam that will take out excess fabric so the container fits loosely in an overall leg.

2   Measure and place a pin 2" from the top edge of the bag in the center front. Place the acrylic board under the center front. Follow manufacturer's directions to install a grommet on either side of the center.

3   Thread cording through the grommets from the wrong side, and tie a knot so the cording will not come back through the grommet. Fold the fabric at the top of the bag under ¼" and then another 1¼" to make the casing. Pin-baste over the cording so you can stitch and not catch the cording. Stitch along the bottom and top edge of the casing using red thread.

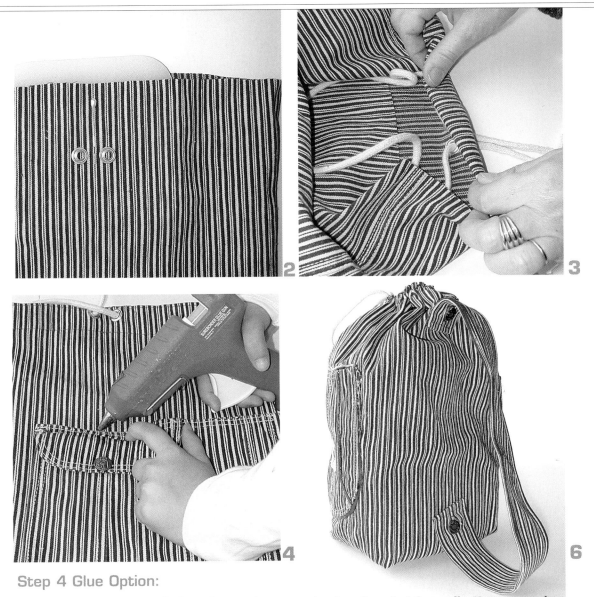

Step 4 Glue Option:

Cut very closely around the large front pockets, removing them from the bib overalls. Next, cut out the side pocket, leaving $\frac{3}{8}$" of fabric at the top of the pocket. Turn fabric back and glue down to finish raw edge. Use clear glue to attach the pockets to the front of the bag $5\frac{1}{2}$" from the top of the bag. Center the pocket with flap under the grommets and wrap the pockets around the side of the bag. Glue the side pocket to left side of bag. When cool, use red glue to outline all pockets and flaps. Cool the bag in your refrigerator to set up the glue quickly.

Step 4 Sew Option:

Cut out pockets as described in step 4. Stitch cording around pockets and then stitch onto the bag $5\frac{1}{2}$" from top, centering pocket with flap under grommets. Stitch the smaller pocket to left side of bag. If fabric is too bulky after attaching cording, you may have to glue the pockets to the bag.

5 Place the plastic container into the bag so the bottom of the container is $2\frac{3}{4}$" from the bottom of bag. Tack in place by putting some glue on the sides of the container. Fold the bottom edges in, sides first, as if wrapping a gift. Glue all edges in place using clear glue.

6 Cut buttons from overalls leaving 1" of fabric on all unfinished edges. Trim away any excess fabric from the back and turn raw edges under, gluing as you go. Fold the strap fabric in half lengthwise. Turn raw edges under $\frac{1}{4}$" on ends and side and pin closed. Stitch all around the strap using red thread. Make buttonholes, lengthwise, on each end $\frac{1}{2}$" from end of strap. Glue buttons to the bag, centering them on back of bag $\frac{3}{4}$" up from bottom of bag and $2\frac{1}{4}$" from top. Button the strap to the bag so it forms a large loop.

Woven Barrel Bag

Materials:

- **12 oz. empty whipped topping container**
- **Denim pant leg to fit container**
- **Denim pocket**
- **Denim waistband button and buttonhole**
- **Approximately 28 belt loops–same length**
- **19" double-stitch seam for handle**
- **1½ yd. red trim**

Supplies:

- **Scissors**
- **Ruler**
- **Glue gun and clear glue**
- **Pins**

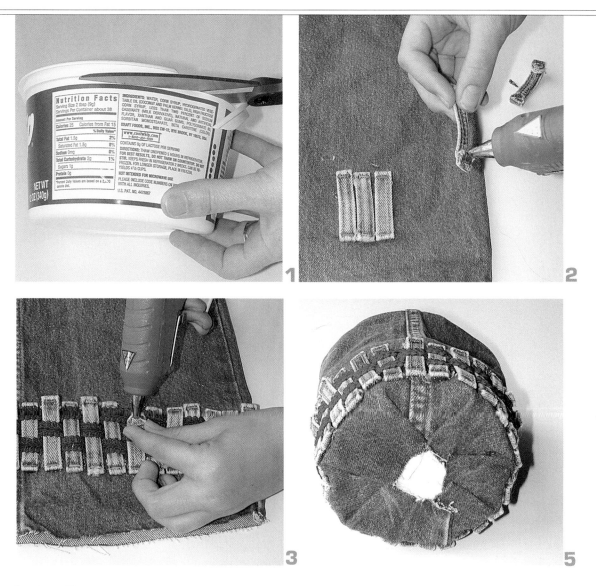

Instructions

1 Cut the rim from the edge of the whipped topping container. Place the container in the pant leg and cut the leg so there is 2" below the bottom of the container and the piece is 9" long, total. Remove the container.

2 Lay belt loops, close together, 2" from bottom edge gluing only the bottom edge of the loops to the pant leg. When all are attached, begin weaving the trim through the loops. Glue the ends of the trim under a loop.

3 Weave three lines of red trim into the loops. Glue the loop tops to the bag.

4 Turn the top edge of the bag under ¼" twice to hide the raw edge. Glue or stitch to hold.

5 Place the container into the bag. Fold pleats into the bottom of the bag so it lays flat to container. Pin in place. Remove pins as you glue pleats. Cut a 4" circle of denim and clip in ¼" all around the edge. Glue or stitch clipped notches to wrong side of circle.

6 Glue circle to the bottom of bag.

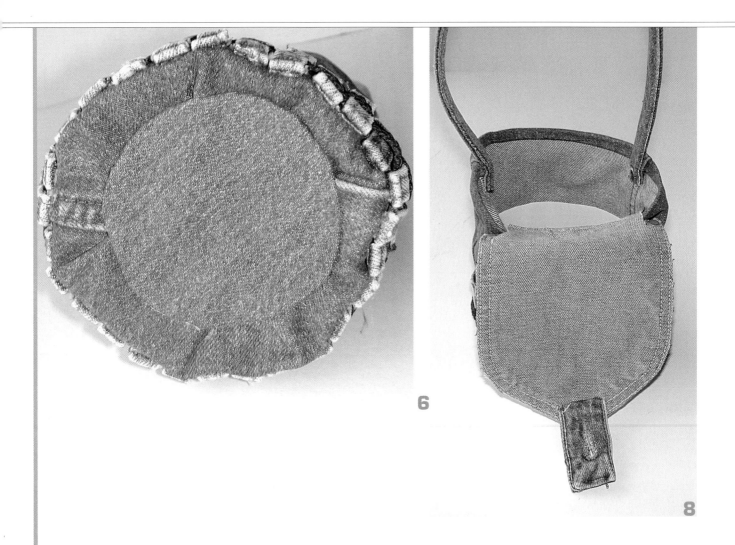

6

8

7   Make sure the pocket has at least ¹/₂" of fabric at the top, behind the actual pocket. Fold raw edge under ¹/₄" and glue or stitch. Attach to the bag by gluing remaining fabric (above pocket) to the back inside edge of the bag. Cut buttonhole and button from waistband 2³/₄" from ends of band. Open cut ends, clip corners, and turn raw edges inside to finish each piece. Put the button in the buttonhole and pin to the back of the pocket. Put glue on the back of the button piece and glue to the side of the bag. Unbutton, and glue the buttonhole end to the underside of the pocket.

8   Make a handle from a 19" piece of double-stitched seam. Fold under the raw edges of the fabric beside the seam, and glue to the back of the seam as described in the Techniques chapter (see page 9). Glue 1" at each end to the inside of the bag at its side.

Spring Pink Barrel Bag

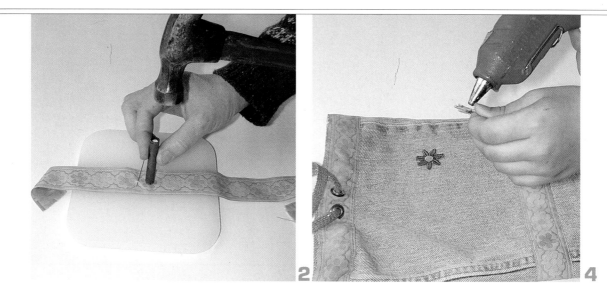

2

4

Instructions

1 Cut the whipped topping container as described in step 1, page 45.

2 Measure 5" from the end of the wide trim and mark with a pin. Install grommets into the trim on either side of the pin following manufacturer's directions. Fold the top of the bag $\frac{1}{4}$" to right side of the bag, cover with trim, and topstitch around the top edge of the bag. Overlap the trim, and turn raw edge under $\frac{1}{4}$" at the end of the trim. Stitch the trim to the trim, but not to the bag, to form a loop. If you stitch the end of the trim to the bag from top to bottom the shoelace will not be able to go through the casing. Lay the shoelace around under the trim and out through the grommets before stitching the bottom edge of the trim to the bag.

3 Stitch the trim to the bottom of the bag so there is 2" of denim below the trim.

4 Cut the flower trim into individual flowers and glue them randomly around the bag.

5 Place the whipped topping container into the bag and finish the bottom of the bag as described in steps 5 to 6, on page 45 .

Flat Purse

Here is a compact
purse that is easy to make,
and it's a trendy party project! You
and your friends each can make a
purse, add your favorite trim or
embellishments, and have a memorable,
new accessory.

Materials:

- ☐ Denim pants lower leg of straight leg jeans
- ☐ 26" double-stitched denim strap
- ☐ Jeans snap, and button
- ☐ Blue bias tape ½" longer than width of purse
- ☐ 2 large Be-Dazzler™ stars
- ☐ Silver-colored glue

Supplies:

- ☐ Scissors
- ☐ Ruler
- ☐ Glue gun and clear glue

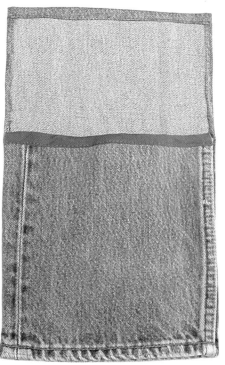

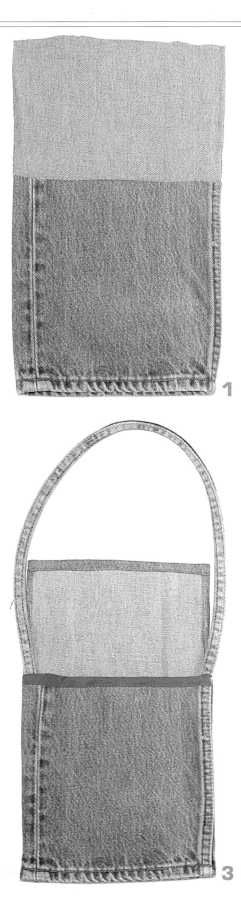

Instructions

1 Cut pant leg 13" up from the hem. Cut down from the top 5½" along side seams. At 5", mark and cut across the front of the leg. (The back of leg above 5" becomes purse flap.)

2 Roll the raw edge on side of flap under so raw edge is hidden, and stitch (or glue). Repeat with the other side and then the bottom edge of the flap. Stitch (or glue) bias tape to raw edge of purse opening by turning the ends of the tape under and stitching in place. Stitch the bottom of the purse closed. If it is too bulky to stitch through the double-stitched seam, glue the bottom of purse closed.

3 Make the strap (see Techniques on page 9) and glue just inside purse on each side.

4

6

4 Cut button and snap each 2½" from end of waistband. Clip corners, trim away any inside seam allowance to remove excess fabric, and fold the raw edges to the inside at open ends. Glue shut.

5 Place button in buttonhole and position on purse (flap closed). Glue button tab to purse and buttonhole tab to the underside of flap. Attach the Be-Dazzler stars according to package directions.

6 Trim can be glued across the bottom edge and around the flap and back of purse for another look.

Slim Purse

Who would guess that this contemporary purse was made from the leg of a pair of jeans? It's a great way to preserve the memory of a favorite pair of jeans by attaching the tags to the handle. A combination of some stitching and some gluing are best for this project.

Materials:

- Jeans leg, 10" wide and 14$\frac{1}{2}$" long
- Jeans waistband
- Jeans fabric for flap lining
- 4 belt loops
- Heavy cardboard 3$\frac{1}{4}$" x 7$\frac{1}{4}$"
- 5 Be-Dazzler 34mm heart studs

Supplies:

- Scissors
- Ruler
- Pins
- Sewing machine
- Thread to match denim
- Glue gun and clear glue
- Be-Dazzler Custom Hand tool

1

2

3

Instructions

1 Cut leg of jeans where it measures 10" across.

2 Cut toward hem of jeans 14½" from first cut.

3 Pleat the side of jeans so that the front and back of the purse is 7½" across. (Note: The 10" end will have a deeper pleat unless jeans are very straight legged.) Stitch along these pleat lines beginning 2½" from bottom of purse and continuing for 8½".

4 Place cardboard in the bottom of the purse—you may need to adjust the size so that the corners of the cardboard are at the ends of pleat stitching.

Step 5 Glue Option:

Fold fabric to form the bottom of the purse—sides first, then front and back flaps—gluing flaps to cardboard as you go.

Step 5 Sew Option:

After folding fabric to form the bottom of the purse, pin-baste in place. Remove cardboard and stitch. Replace cardboard in the purse bottom.

6 To make a flap, cut 3" from top front and sides of the purse, leaving ⅜" on both sides for seam allowance around the flap (so it will be same size as front of purse).

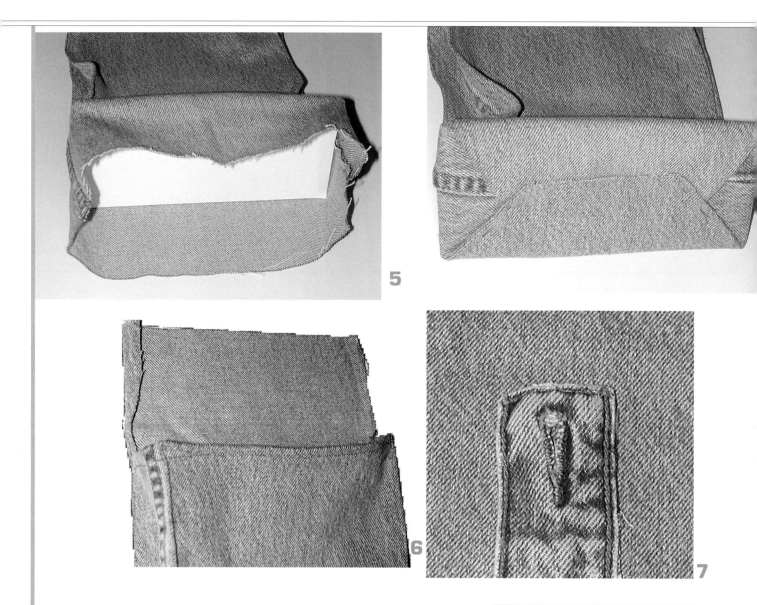

7 Prepare button closure: Cut buttonhole end of the waistband 1" beyond the end of the buttonhole, and ⅝" beyond the button. Rip open the cut end of button tab, and trim away seam allowances. Trim corners off ¼" from end, and turn raw edges in. Glue end closed. Set aside.

8 Cut a piece of denim the same size as the flap piece, adding ½" along the bottom edge to make a lining piece for the flap. Fold raw edge under ½" and stitch. Position the raw edge of the buttonhole piece in the center top of flap.

9 Place right sides of flap and lining together, and stitch around three sides. Trim corners close. Turn right side out.

10 Place button into buttonhole. Fold flap closed and line up button piece so it is square with buttonhole piece. Glue the back of the button piece to purse. (It may be too thick to stitch in place.)

Glue options

Fold seam allowances on flap to wrong side and glue down. Glue buttonhole piece in place. Glue back raw edges of lining piece. Place lining piece over flap, wrong sides together, and glue to each other all around edges.

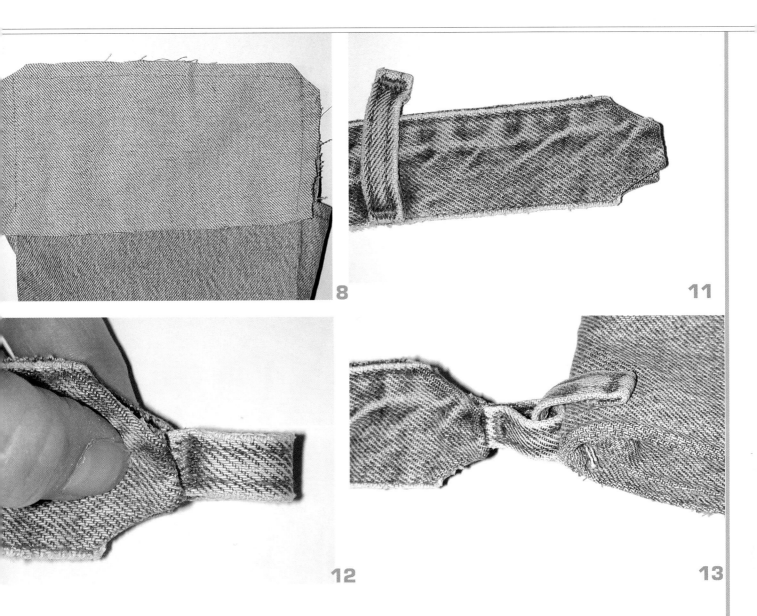

8

11

12

13

11 Prepare handle: Cut 18" piece of waistband, centering belt loops on handle. Cut off any belt loops that are too close to ends. Cut four extra belt loops to use in attaching the handle to purse. (Some belt loops are longer than others, so select the longest you can for these four.) Rip open the ends of the waistband about 1½". Trim off the corners 1", making sure to leave a large enough straight end to cover a belt loop. Fold trimmed raw edges under ⅛", and glue down.

12 Rip open the folded end of two of the belt loops so they are longer. Fold in half and insert into prepared ends of waistband. Glue closed.

13 Put remaining belt loops through the loops at the ends of the waistband. Position on the top of the purse and glue in place.

14 Position five heart studs along the bottom edge of flap. Push prongs through the flap and use the custom hand tool to turn under the prongs.

Suspender Purses

The side pockets are on the back of the purse. Select large enough jeans to ensure that the opening at the top of the purse will be large enough for you to put things into the purse. Both purses can be made by gluing or sewing.

Materials:

- Large jeans
- Suspenders and buttons from bib overalls
- Front from pleated yoke jeans
- 6½" self-adhesive hook and loop, black
- Glue Option: small box with top that is 2" x 9"
- 6¾" double-stitch look denim trim

Supplies:

- Scissors
- Ruler or tape measurer
- Seam ripper
- Pins
- Glue gun and clear glue OR sewing machine and matching thread
- Needle-nose pliers
- Seam ripper

Suspenders from bib overalls make great purse handles that adjust to the length that is just right for you. Look for a pair of jeans that has a wide, straight leg to make the body of the purse. The second style shown uses the front of a pair of jeans with a pleated yoke.

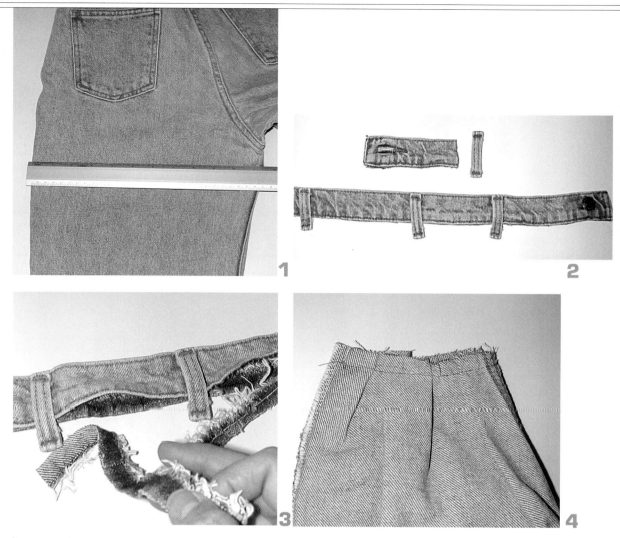

Instructions for Pouch Suspender Purse

1 Cut a piece of pant leg 11" x 9". It is better if the leg is not tapered, but the pleats can make up for some tapering of the pant leg.

2 Cut the waistband from the jeans. Measure and cut 17" from the buttonhole end. Save the button end and at least one belt loop.

3 Use seam ripper to open lower edge of waistband. Remove excess fabric. Form waistband into a circle, overlap end 2¼" behind button end. Tack by stitching along top edge of band or by gluing. Cut back half of waistband where the overlap ends so the waistband will be open to put the bag into it.

Step 4 Quick Sew Option:

Turn the pant leg you'll be using for the bag wrong side out. Form symmetrical pleats on each side and in center so the overall width is 4½". Pin in place and stitch across through all layers.

Step 4 Glue Option:

Glue pleats together and close bottom of purse. Allow to cool thoroughly before turning bag right side out.

5 Turn bag right side out. Pin pleats into the top of the bag so it fits into the waistband. Machine baste around the top of the bag to hold pleats in place. Remove pins.

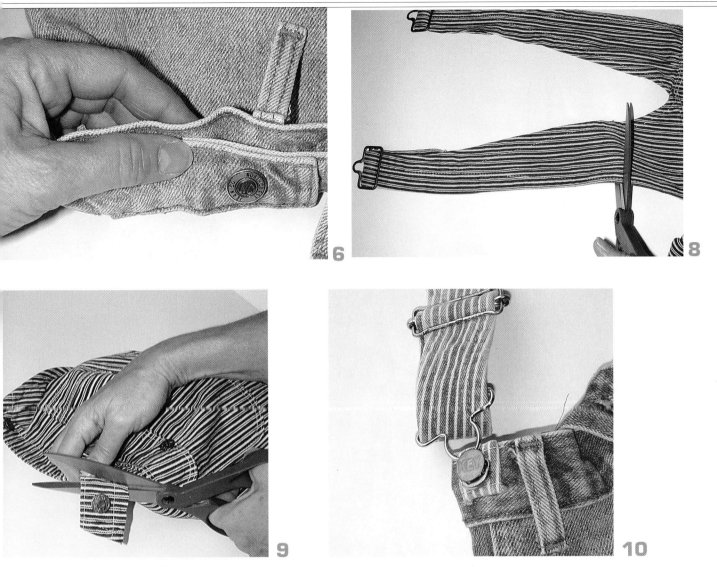

Step 6 Quick Sew Option:

You may try to stitch the waistband onto the top of the bag. It may be too bulky to stitch through in some places. You may have to glue part of it.

Step 6 Glue Option:

Attach the waistband to the bag by gluing the back of the waistband to the wrong side of the fabric, and the front of the waistband to the right side of the fabric.

7 If there is a belt loop in the center of the back where the latch should be, cut the belt loop off. Put the buttonhole over the button and fold it over the back of the waistband to see if it is too long. If it is too long, trim the end to ½" longer than the edge of the waistband. Rip the stitching open 1" at the cut end and remove excess fabric. Clip the corners. Fold in raw edges, and stitch closed. Unbutton the tab, and stitch onto the waistband in the center back.

8 To make handles, cut both suspenders (where they widen to a curve) from the bib overalls. Fold ⅜" of each end to wrong side of fabric. Slide raw edges into folds and flatten. Stitch in a rectangle over the folds to secure.

9 Cut the button from the bib overalls, leaving enough fabric around it so you can fold back all raw edges. Stitch around the outside edge to the hem, or glue edges to the back. Glue to the side of the purse since it would probably be too bulky to stitch it onto the purse.

10 Attach the suspender handles. If the suspender seems like it may fall off, use needle-nose pliers to pinch the buckle together just above the button. This should tighten it so it cannot come off.

Instructions for Pleated-Front Suspender Purse

1 Cut slightly wider than the side seams through the waistband and down 11". Cut across from side to side.

2 Use seam ripper to open each end of the waistband 2". Fold right sides together and trim crotch area so it can be stitched straight down from the zipper.

3 Match edges of the opened waistband and stitch down the side from top to bottom.

4 Trim the bottom edge of the purse straight across. Lay the purse flat, wrong side out, with the bottom edge up. Place a pin at each outside edge. Bring the pins in 1" toward the center to form pleats at the side of the purse. Stitch across this end to close the bottom of the purse. Turn right side out.

5 Put the hook and loop together. Pull off the backing and stick to the backside of the purse opening. Flatten the waistband onto the other side of the hook and loop. Carefully open button and zipper, and cut the hook and loop so the purse can come open. Stitch along the edges of the hook and loop so it will not come loose when the purse is opened. Stitch on the outside, avoiding belt loops and buttons. Close purse.

6 Prepare and attach the handles as described on page 59.

5

6

Glue Options

Keep fabric right side out. Fold one side edge back ⅜" and glue. Lay this edge over the other edge and, placing one end of waistband inside the other, glue closed.. Trim crotch area as described above, and use the same method to glue it closed..To glue the bottom closed, find a small box, such as from cereal, that measures about 2" x 7½" across the top. Place the bag over the box and fold the end of the bag, as if you were wrapping a gift, gluing the fabric as you fold. (Stitching may be easier for this step.)

School Stuff

Covered Notebook

It is so inviting to peek inside this denim-covered journal. It is simple to put together and more than fun to decorate. Surprise!— the spiral binding works well even after it is covered.

Material:

- Paper Reflections Memory Book, 6" x 8"
- Denim for covering notebook
- Double-stitched trim, 6"
- Deja Views® Designer Letters™, red
- VW Bug embroidered patch
- 3 flower buttons
- Red cord, 20"

Supplies:

- Scissors
- Ruler
- Pen
- Pins
- Glue gun, clear glue

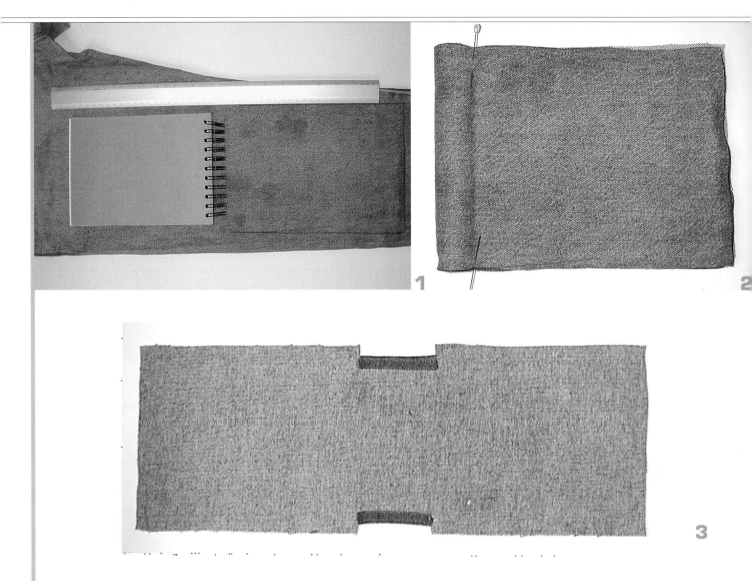

Instructions

1 Lay the journal open onto the denim fabric, and carefully trace around it, adding a ¾" border. Then carefully flip the journal over to the other side, rolling the spiral so it will also be covered. Cut out the denim.

2 Lay denim over the notebook and mark with pins the point where the spiral begins on front and back.

3 Slit in the width of the border and turn denim between pins to inside. Glue down. Cut two pieces of double-stitched trim to cover the raw edges of denim, adding enough to fold edges under on ends. Glue trim in place.

4 Put a line of hot glue just in front of the spiral, then place the notebook onto the wrong side of the denim strip. Press down so the glue holds just beside spiral.

5 Clip corners to ⅛". Put glue on the corner and turn toward notebook ⅛". Glue other edges of the border onto the inside of the notebook cover. Repeat with the other side, making sure there is enough denim to easily cover the spiral area.

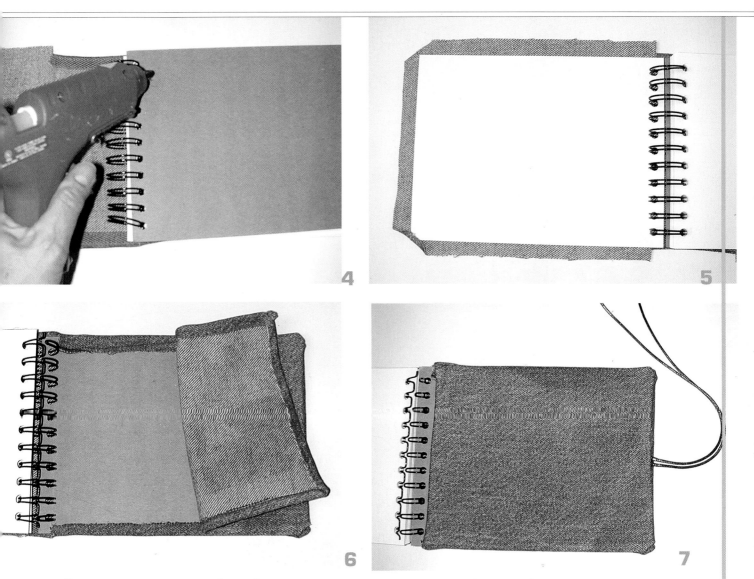

6 Cut two pieces of denim, 8⅛" x 6¼", to cover the inside of the front and back covers. Glue corners toward the center, then turn edges in ¼" and glue down. Check fit, then glue to the inside of the front cover.

7 Prepare the inside cover for the back as described in step 6 . Before gluing it down, cut two pieces of red cord for ties. If necessary, put glue on the ends of the cords to keep them from raveling. Glue the cords at the center of the outside edge of the notebook. Glue the cover in place.

8 Glue the embroidered VW Bug and the three buttons onto the front cover. Place lettering on the cover. Tie cords around the center button to close notebook.

Small Notebook

Materials:

- Notebook
- Denim to cover notebook
- Large pocket
- Belt loop
- Colored hot glue: green, yellow, and purple glitter
- For butterfly antennae: 3 stamens for flowers OR wire

Supplies:

- Non-stick surface for colored glue
- Craft knife or bladed cutter
- Paper punches: 1/8" and 1/4"
- Glue gun and clear glue

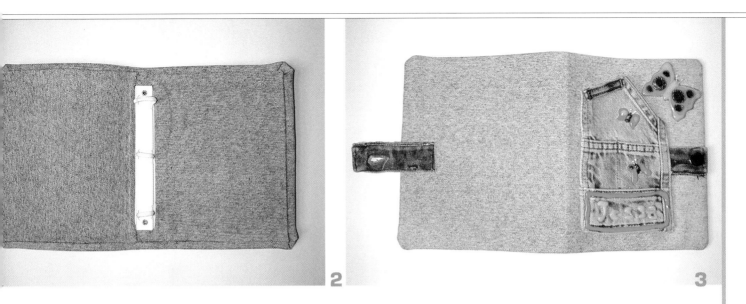

2

3

Instructions

1 This is a ring binder notebook in a small size. Follow the directions on page 64 for the outside cover. You will not need to allow for the spiral, and the cover can be glued to the inside all the way around.

2 Make inside covers as above by taking measurements to fit your notebook. Glue in place.

3 I found a large pocket on a pair of painter-style jeans. Cut around the pocket closely except at pocket opening. Leave enough fabric above the opening to turn back to finish the edge. Glue the belt loop to the top of the pocket to hold the marker in place. Before gluing the pocket to the cover, cut a button from a jeans waistband with 2" of fabric. Glue this so the edge of the pocket will hide the raw edge of the waistband. Cut the matching buttonhole end of the waistband $4\frac{1}{2}$" long. Open the cut end, trim excess bulk, clip corners, and turn raw edges in. Glue the opening closed and put button into buttonhole. Wrap the fabric around to the back of the notebook, and glue the end to the back cover.

4 For colored glue decorations: Use craft knife or bladed cutter to cut four $\frac{1}{16}$" slices from the end of a yellow glue stick. Use punches to make $\frac{1}{4}$" holes in two slices and $\frac{1}{4}$" holes in the other two. Cut slices from purple glitter glue for four $\frac{1}{4}$" circles and two $\frac{1}{8}$" circles. Cut two slices from plain purple and punch two $\frac{1}{4}$" circles. Place the plain circles inside the purple glitter glue holes. Place on the non-stick surface and melt slightly with a heat gun.

5 Using green glue, form bodies for two smaller butterflies and the green part of the large butterfly. Place the dots into the green glue while it is hot. If they do not all melt, heat them carefully with the heat gun. Too much blowing may distort shapes. Cool shapes in the refrigerator a few minutes. Also, make the green frame by applying glue directly to the edge of the lowest pocket.

6 Prepare stamens by cutting in half so there is a pearl end on each piece, or make antenna using thin wire.

7 Spread the yellow glue to form the body and outer wings for the large butterfly. Place prepared green section onto it while the yellow glue is still hot. Add antenna. If desired, make glue letters on non-stick surface. They are a little harder to make so do not try to make them directly on the pocket unless you have practiced first. They can be attached with a little clear glue after they are cold. Finish small butterflies by joining green wings to purple glitter bodies and adding antenna. Use clear glue to attach the large butterfly directly to the cover.

Locker Mate

Denim goes back to school again in this locker organizer. It has just what you need when you're on the go: mirror, pockets for combs, and a place for your pen and note pad.

Materials:

- 8½" x 11" cardboard
- 9½" x 12" denim
- 2 small pockets
- Self adhesive magnetic sheet
- Belt loop
- 3½" x 5" mirror
- Yellow plastic tape
- Post-It® notes
- 21" Wright's trim

Supplies:

- Scissors
- Glue gun and clear glue

Instructions

1 Center cardboard on the wrong side of the 9½" x 12" piece of denim. Wrap the edges to the back and glue to cardboard.

2 Cut plastic tape to the exact length of the top of the mirror. Center tape widthwise along the top of the mirror, and press to front and around to back of mirror to cover edge. Repeat on bottom edge, then on sides.

3 Cut two trim pieces ¾" longer than the top and side of the mirror. Glue side piece to mirror, wrapping ends to back and gluing down. Repeat with piece for top of mirror.

4 The small pockets are "inside" pockets found inside the right front pocket. Some are finished on both sides (as is the top pocket used here). Cut, and trim to fit the length of a belt loop plus enough to turn under to finish the ends of trim. Glue ends under and glue trim to belt loop. Glue the ends of the loop to the small pocket at the bottom of pocket. This will cover, if necessary, the unfinished edge of the pocket. It also provides a place to hook a pen.

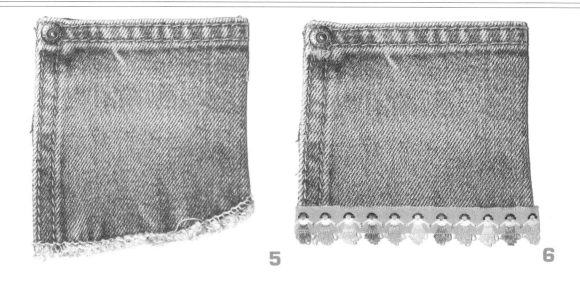

5

6

5   Some "inside" pockets are not finished on one side and bottom. Cut the pocket to 3¾" width or to fit the item you want in the pocket. Trim fabric above the pocket, as in the photo. Fold raw edges on the side and top to the back and glue in place. Cut the bottom of the pocket straight and glue the pocket closed on the bottom. Cover with trim ¾" longer than the width of the pocket so it can be glued around to the back.

6   Cut a piece of trim 11¾" long, and glue it along the right side of the locker mate ¼" from the edge. Arrange mirror, pockets, and note pad as desired and glue them in place. Attach the magnetic sheet to the back following package directions.

Pencil Tote

It's great to have a handy pencil tote to carry your supplies to school. Here's a sporty denim tote with an easy grab handle that can be clipped into a ring binder or even slipped on your wrist. The trim is applied to the flat surface before construction so the possibilities are almost endless. A firm, not floppy, piece of denim works best to hold the shape of the tote.

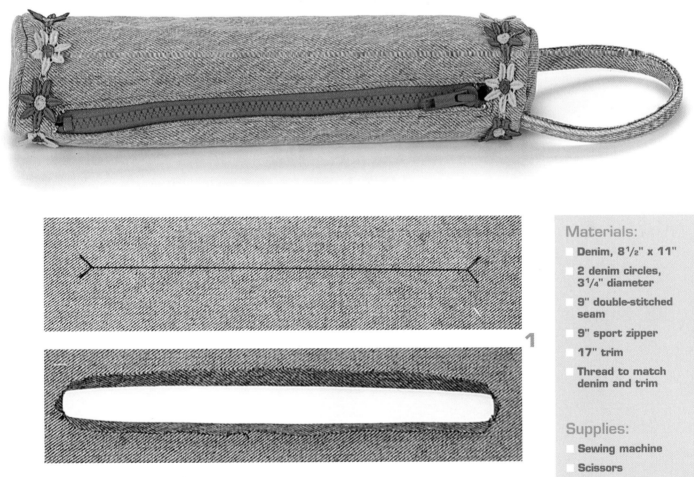

1

Materials:

- Denim, 8½" x 11"
- 2 denim circles, 3¼" diameter
- 9" double-stitched seam
- 9" sport zipper
- 17" trim
- Thread to match denim and trim

Supplies:

- Sewing machine
- Scissors
- Iron
- Pen
- Pins

Quick Sew Instructions:

1   Draw a zipper slit on the wrong side of the 8½" x 11" denim piece. Cut along the lines. Press flaps toward the wrong side of the fabric.

2   Center the zipper in the opening and pin-baste in place. Stitch all the way around the zipper ⅛" from the edge of the fabric.

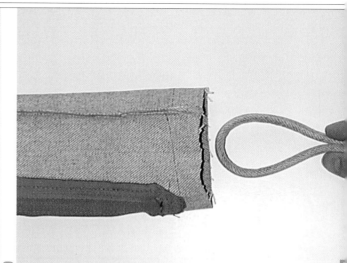

3

5

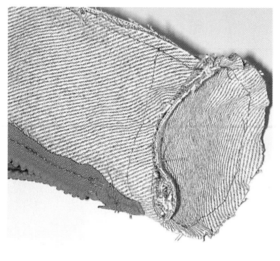

6

3 Stitch trim ½" from the edges of the fabric along the 8½" sides.

4 Fold right sides together along the 11" side and stitch a ¼" seam.

5 Prepare the handle from the 9" double-stitched seam according to Techniques (page 9).

6 Turn the tote wrong side out. Fold the handle in half and place inside the end nearest the zipper tab when the zipper is closed. Baste in place so the handle ends are across from each other forming a large loop. Open the zipper. Place the denim circle with right sides of denim together over the end of the tote. Stitch ⅛" seam all around the circle. Stitch the second circle to the other end in same way. Turn right side out.

Hot Glue Instructions:

1 Draw a zipper slit on the wrong side of 8½" x 11" denim piece, and cut along lines. Glue flaps toward the wrong side of the fabric.

2 Center zipper in the opening (fabric right side up). Lift flap and glue edges down all the way around the zipper.

3 Glue trim in place ½" from the 8½" edges of denim.

4 Fold a flap ¼" wide all along the 11" side and glue down. Glue to other 11" side, overlapping ¼".

5 Prepare a handle from the 9" double-stitched seam according to General Directions (page 9). Turn tote wrong side out and open zipper. Fold handle in half and insert into tote. Glue ends in place on the opposite sides of the tube.

6 Clip circles ⅛" in all the way around, forming tabs. With right sides of fabric together, place the circle in the end of the tube. Glue tabs to the inside of tube. Let set thoroughly before turning tote right side out.

Phone Notes Holder

This handy note holder would make a great gift for almost anyone, and it's so easy to make!

Materials:

- Mat board 6" x 10"
- Denim piece 7" x 11" for front cover
- Denim piece 3/4" x 7 1/2" for strip holding notepad
- Denim piece 6 1/4" x 10 1/4" for back cover
- Small inside pocket
- 6" piece of striped denim from bibs with 2 buttons attached
- 6 3/4" piece of waistband with 2 centered belt loops
- Paper Reflections note pad
- 18" piece Wright's jute cord

Supplies:

- Ruler
- Scissors
- Glue gun and clear glue

Instructions

1 Lay mat board on wrong side of the 7" x 11" denim piece for the front cover. Fold raw edges onto the mat and glue down.

2 Fold the ¾" strip of denim so that the raw edges are turned in, and glue to hold. Position strip 2⅛" from the top. Glue down, except where the note pad will be. Glue the ends of the strip to the back.

3 Clip corners of the back cover. Fold the raw ends along the sides under ½" and secure with glue. Center the cover on the back of the mat, and glue in place.

4 Open the ends of the 6¾" piece of waistband, clip corners of band, and tuck raw edges inside, securing with glue. Do not glue belt loops down yet. Glue band to the top front of the mat.

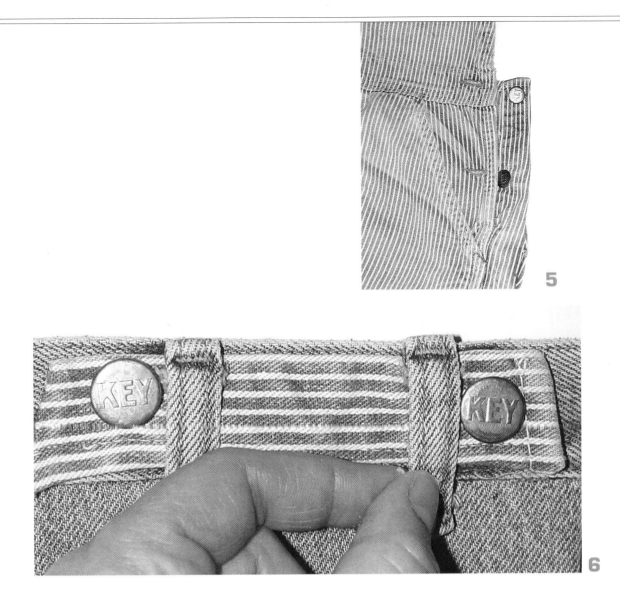

5 Cut the 6" piece from the side of the bib overalls where two buttons are, leaving enough width so you can fold the raw edges under along the length of the piece. Trim the unfinished end at same angle as the closed (top) end. Open the seam at the unfinished end, and trim the excess fabric inside. Clip corners, and turn raw edges inside. Glue closed. Glue the raw edge along the lengthwise edge to the back.

6 Center the strip under the belt loops, and glue in place. Glue the loose ends of belt loops in place.

7 Fold raw edges of inside pocket to back and glue to hold. Glue the pocket onto the mat.

8 Tie jute around the buttons and fringe the ends of the cord.

9 Place a note pad under the strip.

A Denim Christmas

Gift Bags

These gift bags will be the talk of your next party! Gift bags can be made quickly from the bottom of the pant leg of a pair of jeans. It is easier to use straight-legged jeans that are somewhat stiff. The basic construction is the same for these gift bags, but the decoration possibilities are endless ….

Materials:

- Denim pant leg
- Mat board or heavy cardboard 3½" x 6½"
- Denim for handles

Supplies:

- Scissors
- Ruler
- Cutting knife
- Glue gun and clear glue

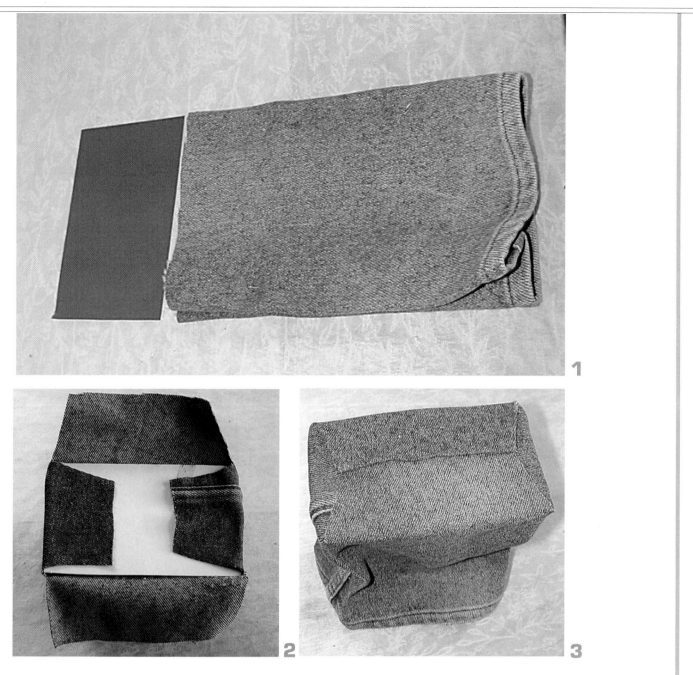

Basic Gift Bag Construction:

1 Measure and cut off the bottom of the pant leg 10½" from the hem. The hem will be used for the top of the bag. Measure the width of the folded leg. Decide how wide the sides of the bag should be and subtract that from the width. These two measurements are the dimensions of the mat board to cut. This will be placed inside the bottom of the bag. Trim or cut the mat board to size. Cut up from bottom edge of bag along each side; fold to make flaps for the bottom of the bag. The length of the cut should be a little more than half of the width of the side of the bag so all flaps will overlap.

2 Glue the bottom side flaps to the bottom of the mat board.

3 Fold all three edges of the last flap of the bag bottom so no raw edges show, and glue in place. If this would make the bottom too bulky so it would not sit well, cover raw edges with trim that looks like a double-stitched seam. This finishes the bottom of the bag.

4 Glue (or stitch) handles to the top of the bag. Specific ideas for handles are given with each gift bag.

Gardener's Gift Bag

Materials:

- Pocket and small pieces from striped denim coveralls

- 22" double-stitched seam for handles

- Button from coveralls

- The Beadery
  - 884A Flower Assortment
  - 1265A Leaf Assortment
  - 4mm white beads

- Surebonder® All Purpose Stik™, approximately 2 sticks

- Surebonder® Jewelry Stik™, 1 stick

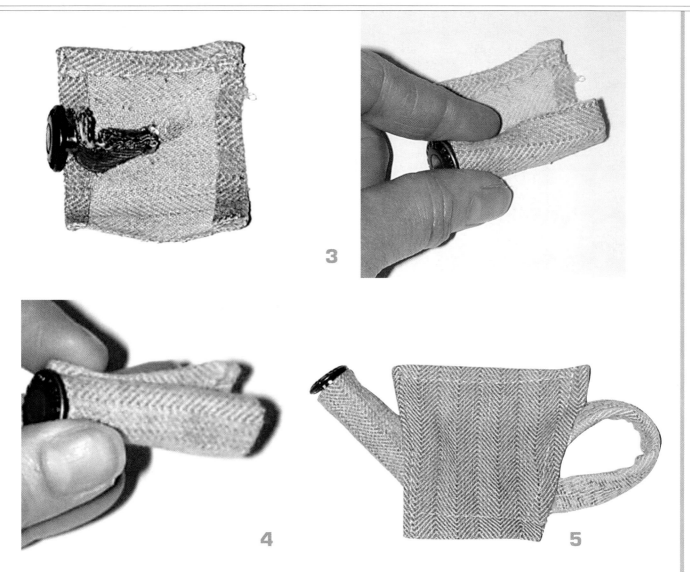

3

4

5

Instructions

1 To make handles for this bag, cut two 11" pieces of double-stitched seam (see Techniques page 9). Fold raw edge under and fold to back of double-stitched seam. Glue down flat. Put glue on end of each handle (½") and glue to inside of bag at corners.

2 This odd-shaped pocket was an inside pocket in a pair of bib overalls. Cut out pocket very close to the folded edges. If you can't find a pocket like this, cut a piece of striped denim 3¾" x 3" and fold and glue edges under to make this shape. Cut a 4" strip of striped denim like the handles of the bag to make the handle for the watering can.

Fold the raw edge under and fold it to the back of the seam; glue down. Glue ends of handle behind pocket.

3 Cut a 2" x 2⅜" piece of striped denim for the spout. Fold under three raw edges and glue down. Glue the shank of the button to the inside center of the spout.

4 Roll it into a tube, folding the raw edge under, and glue the edge closed.

5 Glue the finished watering can to the front of the gift bag about 1½" from the bottom of the bag.

6 Refer to the photo to arrange the bead flowers and leaves. Use Jewelry Glue Stik to attach bead flowers and leaves, and then add round beads in centers of flowers. Use sharp scissors to cut one small green flower to make the small leaves.

Fancy Pocket Gift Bag

Materials:

- [ ] 15" denim waistband
- [ ] 18 gauge wire, 15"
- [ ] 3³⁄₄" x 8" striped denim for envelope
- [ ] 2³⁄₄" double-stitched trim for envelope
- [ ] Red braided trim, 1 yd.
- [ ] The Beadery 18mm round faceted stone, 1 blue
- [ ] Optional: self-stick hook and loop small circle to close envelope

Supplies:

- [ ] Wire cutters

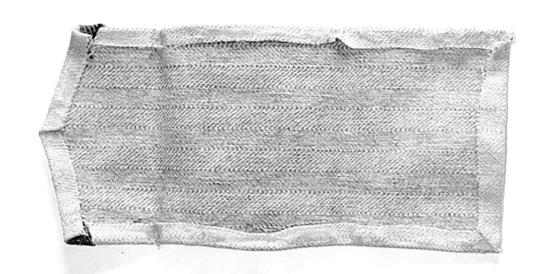

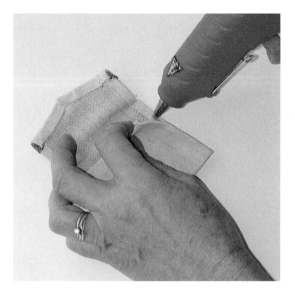

Instructions

1 When cutting waistband for handle, cut so belt loops are centered on the piece. Curl ends of wire and push wire through waistband. This makes it stiff enough to stand up. Lay trim down center of band, through loops, and attach with glue. Glue ends of waistband piece shut and glue to center of bag sides on the inside of the bag.

2 Lay trim in an X on the front of the bag. Glue at corners and center. Glue blue faceted stone over center.

3 Fold envelope fabric in half lengthwise and cut end to a point starting ³⁄₈" from end on side. Unfold and turn all edges in ¹⁄₄"; glue or stitch down. Cut double-stitched trim to fit front. Fold end raw edges under and glue or stitch in place. Fold bottom of envelope up 2¹⁄₂" and fold flap down 2" to create envelope. Glue or stitch sides of envelope closed. If the fabric is soft enough, the envelope will stay closed. If it does not stay closed, add a piece of double stick hook and loop at point of flap. Insert envelope behind top of crossed trim on front of bag.

Striped Heart Gift Bag

Materials:

- 20" striped denim double-stitched seam for handles
- 18 gauge wire, 20"
- 3¹/₂" x 4" striped denim for heart
- Pink piping, 13¹/₂"
- 12" Bucilla 13mm silk ribbon, Variegated Violet Pinks

Supplies:

- Wire cutters
- Iron
- Pins

Instructions

1 Cut double-stitched denim into two 10" pieces. Cut wire to match. Lay wire on wrong side of double-stitched seam. Fold raw edges of fabric beside seam in twice to cover wire and glue down. Fold to curved handle shape and glue ends to inside of bag front and back about 1" from each side. Press silk ribbon with iron and tie in bow at base of front handle.

2 Trace heart from pattern page onto back of striped fabric and cut out. Stitch piping around heart, starting at top center. Fold raw edges to back clipping to make seam lay flat. Glue to front of bag.

Quick Sew Option

Pin-baste and stitch heart to front of bag.

Country Gingham Gift Bag

Materials:

- 20" double-stitched seam for handles
- 4" double-stitched seam for tag
- 4 belt loops
- Jeans tag
- Tan cardstock same size as tag
- 3"-wide gingham ribbon, 26"

Instructions

1 Cut double-stitched denim into two 10" pieces. Fold raw edges of fabric over twice beside seam and glue down. Glue all, but the front right end of each piece, ½" in from side on inside of bag.

2 Cut cardstock slightly smaller than tag. Prepare 4" double-stitched seam as for handles. Fold in half, and glue ends to the back of the tag. Glue cardstock over the back of the tag to hide the ends of the loop. Put remaining handle through the loop, and glue the end of the handle to the inside of the bag.

3 Center two belt loops on the front of the bag and glue down. Repeat on the back. String the gingham ribbon through the loops, and tie a bow in front of the bag.

Sewn Gift Bag Project

This bag is completely sewn, so it can be made a little larger than bags made from a single pant leg. Basic construction of the bag is very easy— and then the fun begins as you embellish it to fit the occasion or use.

Materials:
- Denim
- Cardboard, 9" x 4"
- Colored hot glue

Supplies:
- Scissors
- Ruler
- Sewing machine
- Thread
- Pins
- Glue gun and clear glue
- Craft knife or bladed cutter
- Heat gun

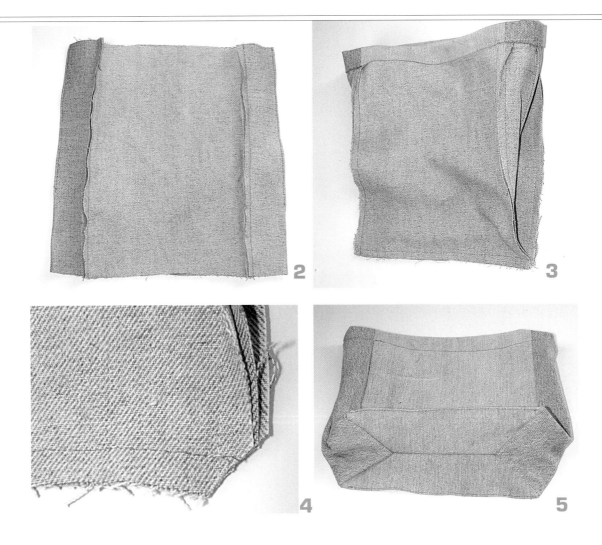

Instructions

1 Cut the following pieces of denim:

Two pieces 9½" x 13" (front and back)

Two pieces 4¾" x 13" (sides for bag)

Two pieces 2⅞" x 18¾" (for straps)

One piece 4¼" x 6⅜" (for patch on front of bag)

2 Fold the side piece in half, right sides together, and stitch ⅛" from edge from top of the bag down to 3" from the bottom of the bag. This makes the center crease in the side of the bag. Repeat with other side piece. With right sides together, match a front to a side piece, and stitch—choose a size of seam allowance and stay consistent (I used ⅜"). Continue joining pieces until all bag pieces are joined.

3 Fold the top of the bag over 1¼" all the way around and pin. Make sure seam allowances are folded open or they will be too bulky to stitch. Fold raw edge under ¼" and stitch all around.

4 Turn the bag wrong side out. Lay the bag flat, folding in the side creases at the bottom of the bag, and stitch across the bottom of the bag. Clip corners at each end of stitching to eliminate bulk.

5 Turn bag right side out, pushing out bottom corners. Stitch ⅛" from edge along each corner of the bag from bottom to top. You may not be able to stitch through hemmed area at top of bag because of bulkiness. In this same way, stitch across the front and back of the bag at the bottom edge.

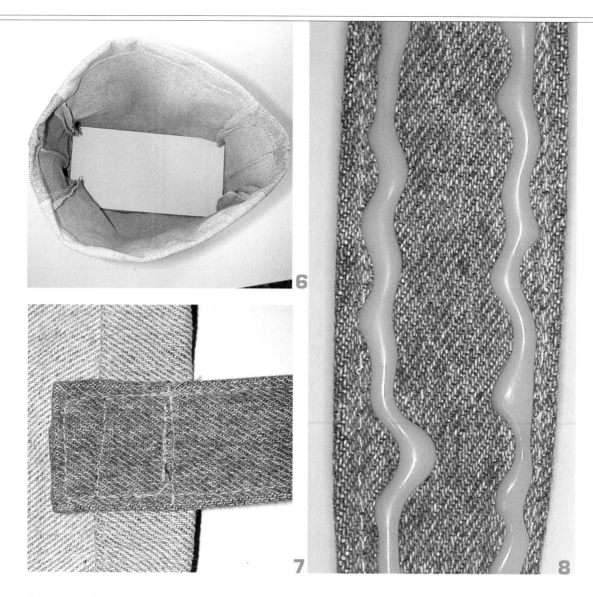

6   Place cardboard piece into bottom of bag to check fit. Remove it and use hot glue to secure it in place. Note: Do not put glue too close to the edge of the cardboard, or it may smear onto the inside of the bag as you push it down into bag.

7   Prepare handles by folding denim in half lengthwise. Fold both raw edges in $\frac{1}{4}$" and pin closed. Also fold ends in the same way so they will be finished. Stitch these edges closed. Topstitch opposite sides of strap the same distance from the edge.

8   Apply colored hot glue to straps up to $1\frac{1}{8}$" from each end. A squiggly line is easier to make than a very symmetrical line. Allow glue to cool thoroughly or place in the refrigerator for a few minutes.

11

9 Stitch ends of straps to inside top of bag by stitching in a square pattern at the end of the handle.

10 Use craft knife or bladed cutter to cut five slices diagonally from orange glue stick Use heat gun to heat fabric a little in the area where the flower petals will be. Place the petals on the denim patch fabric, and heat glue just enough to melt glue onto fabric. Do not hold the heat gun too close to the glue as the force of the air can distort the shape of the petals.

11 Use yellow-colored glue in the glue gun to make the center of the flower and the border. Change to green glue, and make the stem and leaves. When thoroughly cooled, turn the edges of the patch under ¼" and stitch onto the front of the bag.

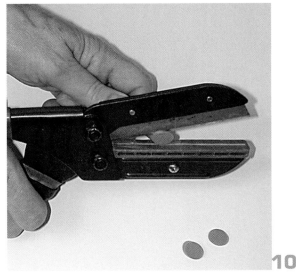

10

Gift Bag Variations

Here are two variations of the sewn bag. Follow the directions for the basic bag. You will also need four small belt loops. Glue one below each strap on the outside of the bag. The first bag has 60" of wired ribbon strung through the loops and tied in a bow.

Gingerbread Man and Holly

The second bag, which matches the Christmas Tree Skirt (see page 94),
uses 26" of cranberry wooden beads strung through the loops.
The following instructions detail the gingerbread man and holly.

Materials:

- Leather Factory Suede Trim

    Medium Brown, 3¹/₂" square

    Hunter green, 4" square

    Suede Lace, white

- Fiebing's Leathercraft Cement

- 2mm black beads for eyes, 2

- Patterns from pattern section, pages 126 and 127

Supplies:

- Scissors

- Pen

- Tracing paper

- Heavy paper

Instructions

1 Trace patterns (pages 126 and 127) onto heavy paper and cut out. Use pen to trace the gingerbread man onto the backside of the brown suede and the holly onto the green suede. Cut out.

2 Cut the following pieces of suede lace: Mouth—⁵/₈"   Eyebrows—³/₈"   Skirt—2"

Put Leathercraft Cement on one edge of suede pieces and apply to the gingerbread man as shown in photo. Glue beads under eyebrows.

3 Use Leathercraft Cement to attach the holly to the bag and the gingerbread man over the top of the holly.

Christmas Tree Skirt

All of these cute gingerbread people will make your Christmas tree skirt
warm and cozy. Since they're made of leather, they will last for years.
The leather also gives a gingerbread-like texture to the project.

Materials:

- 8 denim pant legs
- 40" of denim waistband
- 5⅓ yd. fringe trim
- 3½ yd. blue jean teddy double-stitched trim
- ¾ yd. light-weight polyester fabric for sash, burgundy
- 3 yd. braided cord, gold/burgundy/green
- Leather Factory large suede trim:
  - 6 medium brown
  - 1 hunter green
- 15 Leather Factory Parachute Spots, ⅜" antique nickel
- 12 Leather Factory Parachute Spots, ⁹/₁₆" antique nickel
- Amaco Rub 'n Buff, Spanish Copper and Antique White
- Leather Factory ⅛" suede lace, 6 yd. white
- Feibing's Leather Cement
- Black colored hot glue or 4mm black eyes, 18
- Clear hot glue, 6 sticks
- ½" clear tape
- Thread to match denim and burgundy fabric

Supplies:

- Scissors
- Glue gun
- Ruler
- Pen
- Tracing paper
- Heavy paper or cardstock
- Wooden mallet
- Poly punching board
- Tape measurer
- Seam ripper
- Nail polish remover
- Craft knife
- Acrylic sheet or non stick surface for colored glue
- Paper punches ⅛" and ¼"
- Heat gun
- Needle-nose pliers
- Needle

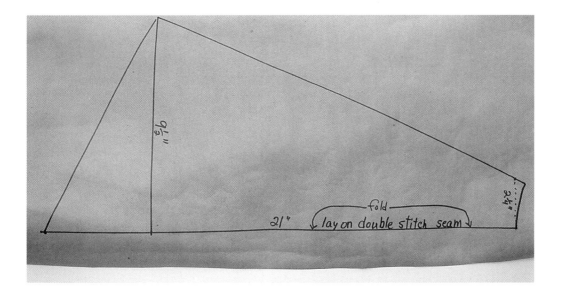

Instructions

1 To make pattern for the skirt sections, draw a 21" base on heavy paper. At one end, mark a point 2¼" to the right of the line. Measure 4½" from other end of base line and mark a point 9½" to the right of the line. Draw a line connecting the end of the base line to the 9½" point and then from point to point. Extend that line (point to point) another ½" and draw a slightly curved line from the baseline to the end of that line. This is half of each section of the skirt, so the baseline can be laid on the seam of the pant leg and one side cut; flip the pattern to the other side and cut around again to make the other half of the section.

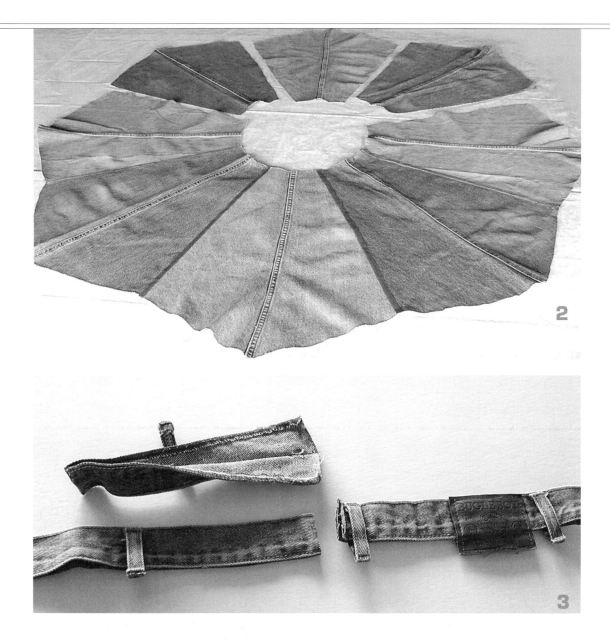

2 Cut eight sections for the skirt. You can alternate light and dark denim to accentuate each section. Lay them out in a circle overlapping each section ½" and glue all but one section to the one next to it. Cut a length of double-stitch trim and glue it over the raw edge on each section. To finish the edges of the two remaining sections, turn raw edges back ½" and glue down.

3 Measure exactly how many inches of waistband is needed for the center of the tree skirt. Use a seam ripper to rip open the bottom edge of the waistband pieces. To add more length to a waistband, cut it in two about ⅜" from a belt loop. Clip corners and trim out excess seam allowance inside the waistband. Cut a section to add on from another waistband. You will lose ¾" from the total measurement because of the splices, so add that to the length of the added section. Open waistband section, apply glue, and push trimmed end of the original waistband into other piece. Repeat at other end of section.

Quick Sew Option

Lay sections, right sides together, and stitch a narrow seam. Place double-stitch trim over the seam on the right side of the denim and stitch it in place. Turn raw edges of the last sections back ½" and stitch.

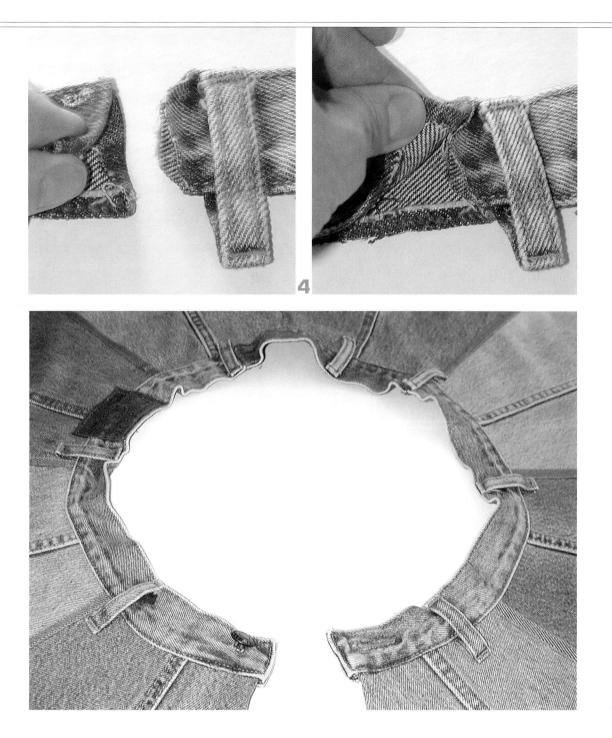

4   Open waistband, and apply glue to one inside edge of the waistband. Lay the top edge of the skirt onto the band over the glue. Continue joining waistband and skirt. Apply glue to the other edge of the waistband and close it over the skirt.

5   Glue loose ends of the belt loops down. Additional belt loops may be needed to hold the sash in place when it is cinched up around the base of the Christmas tree, so glue them, top and bottom, to the band and the skirt.

Quick Sew Option

Pin-baste band onto top of skirt. Stitch through all layers to connect band to skirt.

6 To make gingerbread figures, trace patterns (pages 126 and 127) onto heavy paper or cardstock. Trace around patterns onto backside of brown suede using a pen. You will need four large and five small gingerbread figures. Cut them out.

7 Squeeze a little Spanish Copper Rub 'n Buff onto a scrap of cardstock. Lay the suede right side up on another piece of heavy paper to protect other surfaces. Dip your index finger into a little Rub 'n Buff, and apply it to the edge of the suede using a stroking motion. Go all around the edge of each figure. Clean your finger with nail polish remover.

8 Use the following measurements to cut suede lace for the trim on gingerbread figures:

Man:	Collar—3½"	Side vest—5½"	Adult mouths—⅝"
Child:	Vest side—3¼"	Bow tie—1⅞"	Child mouths—⅝"
Woman:	Collar ruffle—4½"	Apron ruffle—6"	Apron strap—1½"	Legs ruffle—4"

Apply Fiebing's Leather Cement to one edge of the lace and glue it to figure. When set, trim excess from the end of the piece using sharp scissors. To make a bow tie, use the craft knife to cut the ends of the lace at a 35 degree angle. Glue the ends to form a figure eight. When set, glue to gingerbread figure.

14

9   To make eyes from hot glue, spread about a 1" x 2" area of black glue onto an acrylic sheet or non-stick surface. When the glue is cooled, punch sets of eyes: $\frac{1}{8}$" for child, and $\frac{1}{4}$" for adult gingerbread figures. Use the heat gun to melt dots on acrylic sheet or non-stick surface. Heat until just melted and formed into a rounded shape—if you heat them too long, they will spread out too large and become unevenly shaped. Cool thoroughly, and then use Leather Cement to glue to suede. If using purchased eyes, glue them to suede using Leather Cement.

10   To attach parachute spots for buttons, lay the suede figure on poly punching board. Position parachute spot in place and use the mallet to hammer it through the suede. Attach all three at once. Pull suede from board, turn over, and use needle-nose pliers to bend prongs to the outside to keep them from pulling out of suede. If you bend prongs toward the center, it may pull the suede, making it lumpy instead of flat. Apply antique white Rub 'n Buff to the top of each parachute spot.

11   Lay gingerbread figures onto the tree skirt, centering one opposite the opening and laying them approximately 10" apart. Attach using Leather Cement.

12   Beginning at opening, glue or sew fringe around the edge of the skirt, making sure to turn the ends under $\frac{1}{4}$" to prevent raveling.

13   Trace the pattern for holly and then trace onto the back of the hunter green suede in the same manner as you did for the gingerbread figures. Cut out, apply Leather Cement to back and glue in place on skirt.

14   To make candy berries, put tape on the end of the cord. Lay the cord on a ruler and put a piece of clear tape across the cord and ruler at the 6" line. Cut in the middle of the tape at the 6" line so both ends of the cord are held from unraveling. Remove the cord from the ruler, and tie a knot near one end. Glue end near knot underneath so it doesn't show. Wrap other end of cord around into a tight circle applying hot glue to hold, ending with the second taped end under the circle. You will need 27 of these. Glue one in the center of the holly leaves and the other two randomly around each gingerbread figure.

15   To make the sash, cut three strips of lightweight polyester fabric 8$\frac{1}{2}$" x 34". Lay fabric, right sides together, and stitch along 8$\frac{1}{2}$" ends to join all three pieces. Fold in half, right sides together, to make a 4$\frac{1}{4}$" x 100" strip. Stitch closed, angling ends to a point and leaving a 5" gap in stitching so you can turn it right side out. Trim corners and ends to remove excess fabric. Turn right side out. Hand stitch opening closed and press sash flat. String through belt loops and tie in a bow.

Gingerbread Tree Ornaments

Materials:

- Materials to make small gingerbread figures described on pages 94 through 99
- Therm O Web Heat 'n Bond® Ultra Hold Iron-On Adhesive
- Ornament hook
- Denim

Supplies:

- Iron
- Ironing board
- Pen

Instructions

1 Prepare small gingerbread figure as described on page 98. Cut a 13" x 6" striped or blue denim piece. Cut Iron-on Adhesive 6½" x 6". Follow manufacturer's instructions to bond the adhesive to half of the denim on the wrong side of the fabric. Fold the other half of denim piece over, and place the ornament hook in what will be the top; bond so the right side of the denim fabric shows on both sides.

2 Place gingerbread figure upside down on prepared denim and trace around, making a border approximately ⅜" larger than figure. Cut on traced line. Use Leathercraft Cement to glue figure to other side of denim cutout.

Candy Cane Ornament

Materials:

- Denim and iron-on adhesive
- Cord and double-stitched trim described above
- Glue gun and hot glue
- Clear adhesive tape

Instructions

1 To make the candy cane ornament, prepare a piece of denim, 8" x 2" when unfolded, with ornament hook as described on page 101. Cut a 4½" piece of cord with a small piece of tape on each end to prevent raveling. Cut a 1" piece of double-stitched trim. Fold one end under ⅛" and glue.

2 Wrap and glue other end around end of cord finishing with folded end to cover end of cord. Repeat on other end of cord. Trace around cord as described for gingerbread figure, or just glue cord to denim piece and then cut around it ⅜" from cord.

Christmas Ball Ornament

Complete the denim Christmas look with these large ball ornaments. The copper colored hot glue appears to be dripping like melted chocolate. If the glue is very hot in the glue gun, it will run more quickly. Cooler glue looks more mottled. The glue stays warm for quite a while because it is thick. Be careful not to touch the warm glue or drop the ball, as it will stick to things until it has been chilled.

Materials:

- [ ] 5" Plastifoam® ball
- [ ] 8½" x 16½" piece of denim
- [ ] 7" denim seam for hanger

Supplies:

- [ ] Scissors
- [ ] Glue gun and clear glue
- [ ] Pins
- [ ] Mug or drinking glass
- [ ] 8 colored glue sticks, copper

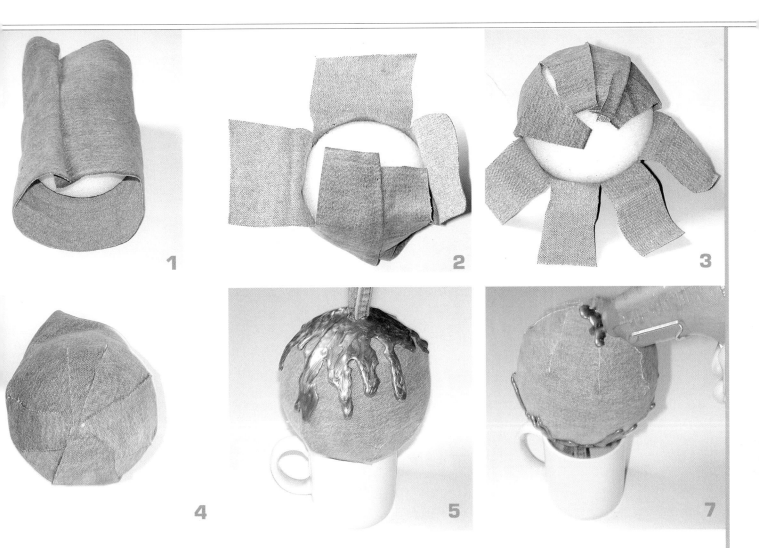

Instructions

1 Cut denim so there is a double-stitched seam in the center of the length of fabric if you wish to have a seam around the center of the ball, or cut so there is no seam for a smooth effect.

2 Wrap the ball in the denim, folding the raw edge under along the edge that will be on top. Tack down with clear glue. Pins may be placed around the equator of ball to keep the denim from slipping while you smooth the denim in place. Remove them when finished.

3 Cut slits in the denim to allow you to smooth the denim down to fit the ball. Raw edges do not have to be turned under, and excess fabric should be cut away.

4 Use clear hot glue to close seams, overlapping denim slightly.

5 To make the handle, cut a 7" piece of double-stitched seam as described in Techniques (page 9). Turn raw edges under and fold piece in half. Use copper colored hot glue to attach handle to top of ball where denim pieces meet. Let the glue set up around the handle.

6 Hold the ball carefully and firmly while spreading copper-colored glue down from top of ball. Be sure to cover all seams and make other "drips" of glue as desired between seams. Glue will remain tacky until it is dry, so be careful not to touch or drop the ball during this time. Set the ball on a mug or drinking glass and place in refrigerator for a few minutes to set the glue.

7 Remove ball from refrigerator, hold or set on mug while you repeat spreading colored hot glue on the opposite side of ball. Chill to set.

Gifts and Things

Shaving Tote

A shaving tote is a must for every man, so this would make a great gift for everyone from the graduate to a grandfather. It goes together quickly and works best with very straight-legged jeans that are fairly stiff. If you can't find straight-legged jeans, the directions explain how to make adjustments.

Materials:

- 12" bottom of leg of jeans
- 5" x 6" denim
- 10" double-stitched seam for handle
- 9" zipper

Supplies:

- Ruler
- Scissors
- Pins
- Sewing machine
- Thread
- Glue gun and clear glue

Instructions

1. Cut a pant leg 12" from the hem, and trim off the hem. If the leg is not straight, rip open the seam that is not double-stitched. Place right sides together and measure the narrow end. Pin-baste in a straight line using the narrow measurement to make the line. Stitch seam.

2. Hold the end in a dome shape. Measure across the bottom to the center top. Cut two rectangles to these measurements. The leg I used was 7½" across when laid flat. I cut a rectangle 6" x 5". Cut the top of the rectangle into a dome shape.

3. Center the zipper along the double-stitched seam. Mark the ends of the actual zipper (not tape) with pins. Remove the zipper. Cut very close to the seam from pin to pin.

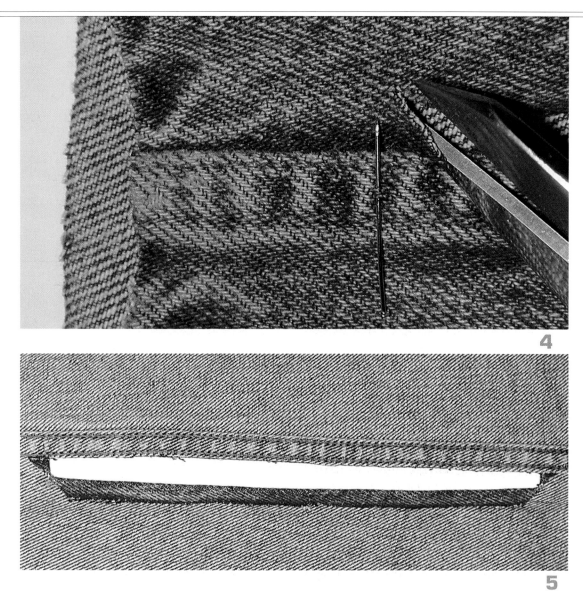

4

5

4 Make a cut ⅜" back from each pin at a 45 degree angle to a point even with the pin. Remove pins.

5 Turn tote wrong side out and glue flaps down. Turn right side out and position the zipper behind the opening. Glue in place.

6 Prepare a 10" strip of double-stitched handle (see page 9). Glue ends of the handle to the end of the tote just above the zipper tab, making sure the double-stitching is facing the right side of the tote fabric.

Quick Sew Option

Press or stitch flaps open. Pin-baste the zipper in place and stitch around all sides of the zipper.

Quick Sew Option

Stitch ends of handle in place as shown in photo.

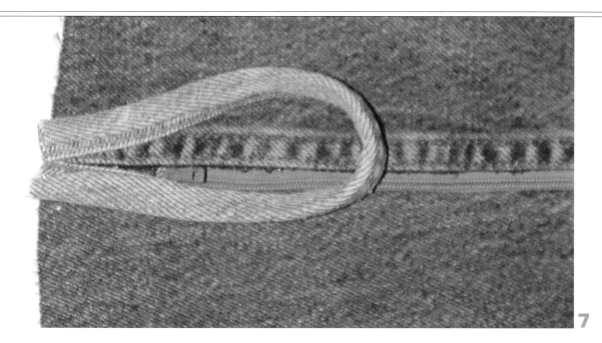

7

7 Center the dome-shaped end piece over the seam, right sides of fabric together. Stitch ⅜" seam to within ⅜" of each end. Clip through both layers of fabric at ends of stitching. Turn the tote wrong side out. Check the fit of the dome to the end of the tote and pin-baste in place. Stitch over the top of the dome to close the end of the tote. Open zipper. Repeat with other end of tote. Turn right side out.

Hot Glue Option

Position the end piece over the seam and glue in a straight line ⅜" from edge. Clip through both layers of fabric at ends of gluing. Check the fit of the dome, and clip curved edge in about ⅜". Open zipper and turn tote wrong side out. Glue tabs down around end, gluing all around. Stuff the end with rolled up cloth to give you something to push on.

Covered Frame

Introduce denim into your home décor with this frame. The relaxed look compliments country or casual styles well, but could serve as a conversation piece in any room. The waistband embellishment gives a more masculine or casual look while the braided denim seems a bit more feminine. The foam base allows either embellishment to be attached with pins so it can be changed at any time. The cover for the frame can be glued onto the foam base or stitched and then wrapped around the base. Gluing can give a tighter, more precise fit. Stitching the cover requires very accurate cutting and stitching.

Materials:

- Plastifoam frame: 12" x 17" x 2" x 2"
- Denim pieces to fit pattern
- 2 jeans waistbands *or* 2 braided strips using six 30" pieces of double-stitch seam
- 8 belt loops
- Belt loop for hanger
- 4 large head pins such as corsage pins

Supplies:

- Craft knife
- Ruler
- Scissors
- Pins
- Glue gun and clear glue
- Sewing machine
- Thread

Instructions

1 To make an indentation where you will insert your photo or artwork: Use a ruler and craft knife to cut a notch ½" x ½" from the inside edge of the back of the frame.

2 Cut two of the pattern on page 128.

Step 3 Glue Option:

Place the larger piece on the long side of the frame. Pull the denim around to the indentation on the inside edge of the frame and glue along the indentation. Pull the opposite side of the denim around the back of the frame to the other edge of the indentation, and glue in place along that edge. Pull ends over corners and tack down with glue or pins. Repeat with the second large denim piece on the opposite side of the frame.

Step 3 Quick Sew Option:

Lay the smaller piece over the larger piece, right sides together and matching notches, and stitch between large dots on the pattern. Clip corners and trim one seam to half the width of the other seam to eliminate bulk. Repeat on the other set of sides. Join these sets at one corner, but do not stitch last corner together fully or you will not be able to pull it over the frame.

4 Place the smaller piece of denim on one remaining side of the frame. Tack denim, with glue or pins, in the indentation in center of back. Fold raw edges under at corners to form a mitered corner. Glue in place. Finish gluing edges in the indentation as on long sides. Repeat with remaining smaller piece.

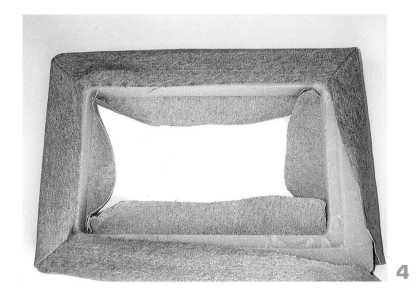

4

5 Turn fabric right side out and pull it over the frame. Hot glue raw edges into the indentation in the back of the frame, starting in the center of each side and working to the corners. Glue the last corner closed, overlapping fabric as described for glued option.

6 Cut waistband and belt loops from jeans, leaving loops attached to waistband. Cut very close to waistband seam. Cut 17" from button end and 13" from buttonhole end. Open cut ends and tuck raw edges in. Glue or stitch closed. Put button in the buttonhole and lay both sets on the frame, tucking ends under on opposite corners. Glue or pin in place. Glue or pin loose ends of belt loops to the inside of frame.

5

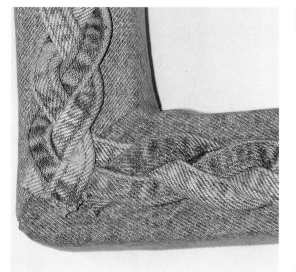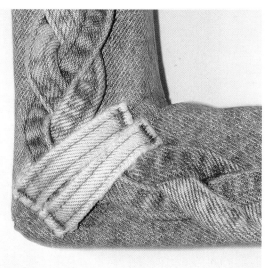

7 Position a belt loop horizontally in the center of the topside of the frame, and glue firmly at both ends of the belt loop. This forms a hanger for the frame. Use long pins with large heads to hold artwork in the frame.

Braided Option

Construct braid by preparing six 30" strands of double-stitch seam as described in the Techniques chapter (page 9). Begin braiding them, holding strands together with hot glue at the beginning of each set. Glue strands together to hold ends when finished. Each braid fits along one side and one end. Overlap the ends of the strands, making them as flat as possible. Pin or glue braid at the ends and in the middle of each side. Pin or glue two belt loops over each corner to hide braid ends and give a finished look.

7

Covered Tin

Make this project using a tin with a plastic lid that snaps on, like a coffee can or soup mix tin. With this technique, you can create a container embellished in any style. And when you're done, fill the tin with his favorite goodies, and voila!—it's a great gift for dad.

Materials:

- Denim to cover tin and lid
- Leather trim, 2" x 12"
- Lip Cord trim, Light Blue
- Double-stitched trim or double-stitched seam, twice the circumference of tin
- Quilt batting to fit lid top
- $^3/_8$" grommets, 2
- Fiebing's Leathercraft Cement

Supplies:

- Scissors
- Tracing paper
- Pen
- Pins
- Grommet kit
- Craft knife or leather tooling tools
- Glue gun and clear glue
- Hammer
- Acrylic cutting board
- Cellophane tape
- Black paint pen or permanent marker

Instructions

1. Remove the canister label, and position it on denim so the grain of fabric is straight with the edge of label. If you don't have a paper label, measure the height, below the lid, and the circumference of the tin. Add $^1/_2$" to height and $^3/_4$" to circumference so you will be able to fold raw edges back and overlap around the tin. Cut out denim to these measurements. If you are using actual double-stitched seam as a trim, line the label up with a seam at the lower edge of the label, adding enough to the other side of the seam to turn under to make a finished edge. Add $^1/_4$" to top edge and $^3/_4$" to end, and then cut out.

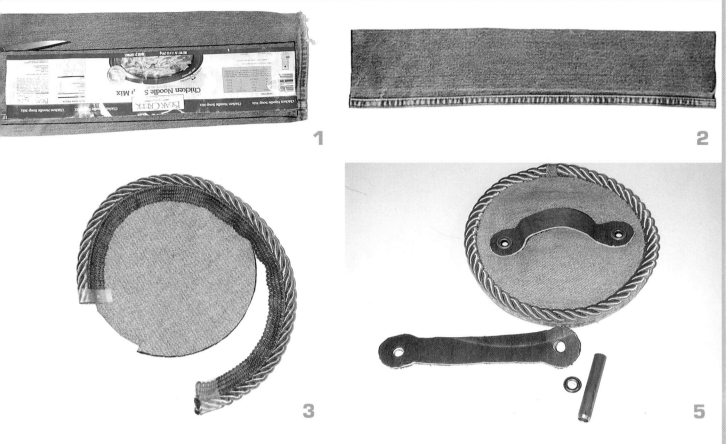

2 Turn raw edges under ¼" on long edges of denim, and glue or stitch to back. Cover with double-stitched trim on the edge that will be along bottom of tin. Turn denim back ⅜" at one end and glue. Wrap denim around the tin overlapping ends. Pin in place and check the fit of the lid to make sure denim does not extend too far up on tin. Glue denim to denim where it overlaps to hold it around the tin.

3 Place the lid on the wrong side of denim, and trace around it. Cut out and snip all around edge in ³⁄₁₆". Turn tabs under and glue down. Measure lip trim to fit around lid. Tape ends of cording where you cut it so it will not ravel. Clip lip edge of trim every ½" and glue lip around edge on backside of denim circle. Cover ends of trim with a small piece of double-stitched trim.

4 Cut quilt batting to fit on top of the lid and tack down with hot glue. Tack denim to the batting, making sure edges match the edge of lid.

5 Trace pattern for handle onto back of leather trim. Cut out handle and use grommet tools to make holes in leather. Make holes for grommets in lid through all layers. These holes should be close enough together to make handle raised up in center. Install grommets according to package directions. Glue batting layer to lid. Glue cord to lid. Measure a length of double-stitch trim or double-stitched seam to fit around edge of lid and glue it around the side of the lid.

6 Trace patterns for decorations on page 126 on side of tin onto back of leather trim and cut out. To make detail lines on cutouts trace lines onto leather, moisten it a little with water, then cut lines with craft knife or leather tools removing a little of the top of the leather. Add color details with black permanent marker or paint pen. Use Feibing's Leathercraft Cement to attach cutouts to denim.

Reversible Photo Frame

Materials:

- Cardboard or mat board 1- 6" x 8"
- Denim to cover cardboard
- Elastic trim 38½"
- Non-elastic trim 22"

Supplies:

- Scissors
- Ruler
- Craft knife
- Glue gun and clear glue

This versatile frame puts another touch of denim in your décor. Either side can be used to display your favorite snapshot. Since it is super simple to make, it would be a good project for kids of any age. Use cardboard that is thin, yet firm. Mat board is great and scraps may sometimes be obtained from a framing shop. Striped bib overall denim on one side makes an interesting background, but may be too "busy" for some photos. Let your imagination go when it comes to trim. A more elegant look can be achieved by using lace or satin cording. Elastic under the ribbon trim eliminates the need for actual elastic trim.

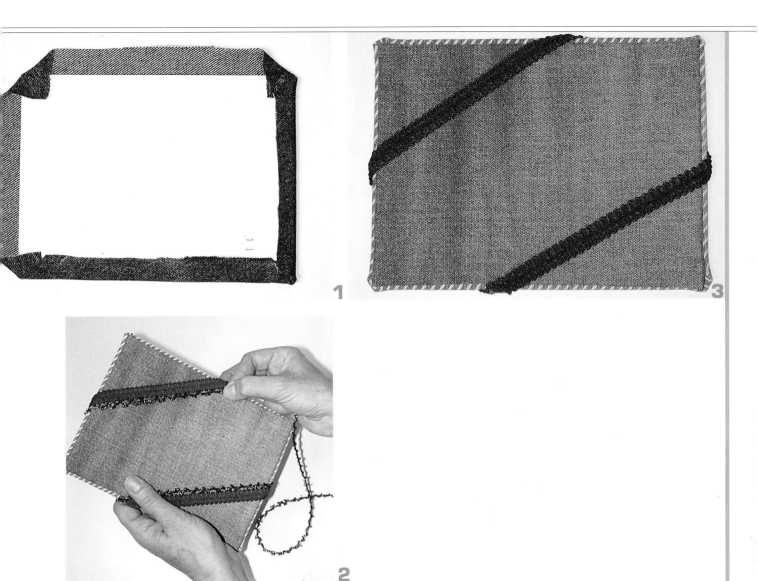

Instructions

1 Cut denim so there is a ¾" border all around the cardboard. First, glue corners down. Next, glue the fabric between corners until all edges are glued to back of cardboard. Repeat with striped fabric on other piece of cardboard. Center the smaller board over the wrong side of the larger board and glue the two together.

2 Glue end of trim to board about 2½" from a corner along the top edge and begin to wrap trim diagonally around board. Glue at edges to keep it from slipping, and glue end slightly overlapping the starting point of trim. You may need to turn the end of the trim under to hide the raw edge.

3 Glue end of elastic trim just under the edge of the first trim piece near the edge. Begin wrapping trim next to other trim. Finish by gluing end under edge again. Repeat with trim on opposite side of first trim piece.

Corded Frame

This frame shows a more elegant look using lace or ribbon and satin cording. If you wish to use the frame in a portrait position just repeat the cording pattern that is on the top of the frame on the opposite side also. Then the two sides will match. Also, cut both pieces of cardboard the same size since you do not want the edge of the first to show behind the smaller board.

Materials:

- Cardboard and denim as above
- 14" narrow elastic
- 10" ribbon
- 10" lace
- 30" satin cording with lip edge

Instructions

1 Follow the directions on page 119 for covering the boards with your choice of shades of denim.

2 Check to see if two pieces of elastic, each 4½" long, will cover the corner of the photo. Glue the elastic to the back of the board 2½" from corner. Stretch elastic a little as you glue the other end to a point 2½" down from the corner. Cut ribbon to cover the elastic. Leave the ribbon just a little loose as you glue it over the elastic on the back of the board. Repeat at opposite corner.

3 Follow the above directions to attach the elastic and lace to the other board.

4 On the back of one of the boards, cut a 6" piece of satin cording and position it in the center of the top of the board with the ends curved down toward the center of the board.

This will hide the raw ends of the trim. Glue trim in place.

5 Glue the remaining cording around the board, curving the ends down as close as possible to other ends. Make sure the lip of the cording does not show around the edges of the board. Glue the other board, right side up, over back of this board.

Belt Loop Basket

This lined basket will show you an easy and quick way to achieve the woven look using belt loops. The height of the basket will be determined by the length of belt loops you find—they do vary in length by the size of the jeans and by the brand. This basket measures about 6½" by 3½" and is 2⅝" tall. It took fourteen belt loops for the uprights and thirty-five belt loops going around the basket. There are usually five or sometimes six belt loops on each pair of jeans. A variety of shades of color used together is fine. Any cardboard or papier mâché box that is the right height is suitable.

Materials:

- Cardboard or papier mâché box as tall as longest belt loops
- Belt loops to cover box
- Denim for lining and handle
- Cardboard to fit bottom of box
- Thread to match top stitching on loops
- 18 gauge wire

Supplies:

- Glue gun and clear glue
- Scissors
- Tape measure
- Pen
- Craft knife and straight edge
- Sewing machine
- Wire cutters

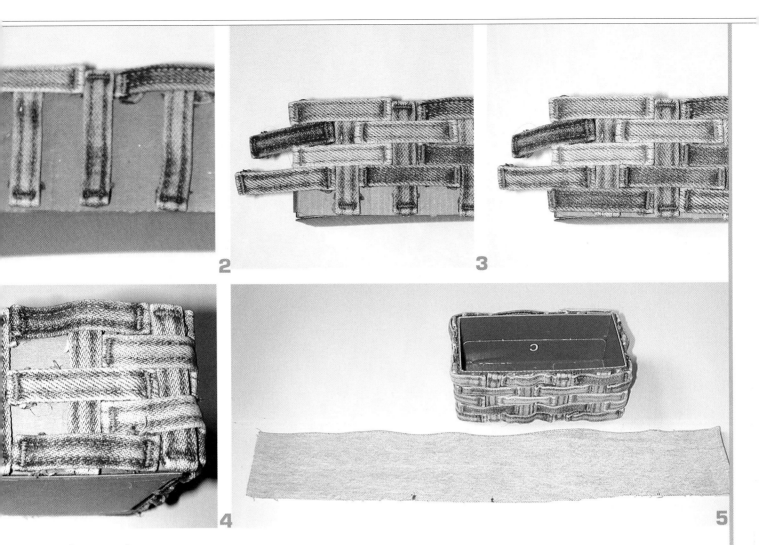

Instructions

1 If the box is too tall, mark the desired height with pen and cut box using craft knife and straight edge. See Techniques (page 11) for tips on removing belt loops from jeans.

2 Begin arranging belt loops on one side of the box, placing an upright loop under the center of each horizontal loop and between each one. Center the horizontal loops so the corners will not have an upright loop on the corner. Glue the first row in place.

3 Continue adding horizontal belt loops. Do not glue the ends that go around a corner until you have secured the sides.

4 Upright loops can be right next to the corner. You may need to use slightly longer or shorter loops on the ends so you can center the upright loops at each corner and in the center of the end of the box. It is best to have opposite sides the same—belt loops exactly across from those on the opposite side. This will make the whole basket look uniform. Adjusting the size of the loops on the ends allows you to do this. The last loop completes the puzzle.

5 Use the tape measure to find the circumference and depth of the inside of the basket. Add ¾" to the circumference and 1" to the depth. Cut a piece of denim for the lining using these measurements. Other fabric could be used for another look. Turn the top edge under ¼" and stitch. Turn one end under ⅜" and stitch. Measure and mark the length of each side and end on the lining so you will know where the corners will be when the lining is placed into the basket. Cut a slit ⅜" long at each corner mark. This will allow the fabric to lay flat when it turns a corner.

6 Place the lining into the basket and arrange so the corner slits are at corners and the fabric covers the top edge of the box. Glue the lining in place, starting with the unhemmed end. Spread glue along the top and a little on the first side. Smooth that side in place. Repeat with all sides and the end by overlapping the hemmed end over the beginning end.

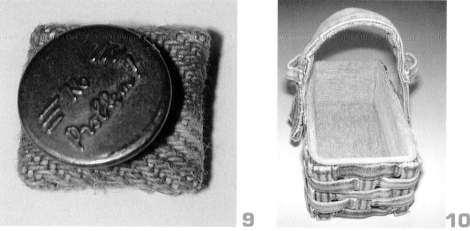

Quick Sew Option

Before inserting the wire into the handle, stitch another buttonhole on the open end of the handle far enough from the end so the end can still be closed. Cut the loop off the end of the wire and push the wire into the handle. Fold the raw edges of the end in, and stitch closed. Then find a second button and prepare it like the first one, putting it into this buttonhole. When you glue just the buttons onto the side of the basket the handle will be able to fold down.

7   Cut a piece of cardboard to fit a little smaller than the inside bottom of the box.

Cut a piece of denim ½" all around cardboard. Clip corners. Glue the flaps that are formed to the back of cardboard piece. Turn it over and glue it inside the bottom of the box.

8   Cut a piece of waistband with a button at one end, and belt loops that are centered from each end to make a suitable handle when bent into a U shape. Trim the cut end by clipping edges, opening the bottom edge slightly, and removing excess fabric. Use wire cutters to cut a piece of wire the length of the waistband, and curve one end unto a U shape. Push the wire into the waistband. Turn the raw edges of the open end to the inside, and glue it shut. Glue the loose ends of the belt loops on the handle to the edge of the waistband.

9   Cut the button from the original waistband, along with about a square inch of fabric around it. Fold all of the edges to the back, and glue them down. Place the button in the buttonhole before deciding where to glue it to the basket.

10   Curve the handle and center it on the side of the basket. Glue the back of the button to the basket on one side and the end of the handle to the basket on the other side.

Note: When positioning the handle to basket, make sure the belt loops on the handles are both the same distance above the sides of the basket.

Resources

Amaco
4717 W. 16th St.
Indianapolis, IN 46222-2598
(800) 374-1600
(Rub 'N Buff®)

The Beadery Crafts Products
106 Canonchet Rd.
Hope Valley, RI 02832
www.thebeadery.com
(Faceted Stones, Flower Assortment, Leaf
Assortment)

C-Thru Ruler Company
6 Britton Dr.
P.O. Box 356
Bloomfield, CT 06002
(Deja Views® Acid Free Designer Letters)

Delta Technical Coatings, Inc.
2550 Pellissier Pl.
Whittier, CA 90601
(800) 423-4135
www.deltacrafts.com
(Ceramcoat paint)

DMD Industries, Inc.
The Paper Reflections Line
1205 ESI Dr.
Springdale, AK 72764
(800) 805-9890
(Paper Reflections Memo Pad and Memory Book)

Fairfield Processing
88 Rose Hill Ave.
Danbury, CT 06810
(Pillow inserts)

FPC Corporation
355 Hollow Hill
Wauconda, IL 60084
(800) 860-3838
www.surebonder.com
(Surebonder® Glue Guns, Surebonder® Sure Stik,
colored hot glue)

The Leather Factory & Tandy Leather
Company
3847 E. Loop 820 S.
Fort Worth, TX 76119-4388
(800) 433-3201
(Suede trim, suede lace, parachute spots,
Leathercraft Cement)

Midwest Products Co, Inc.
400 Indiana St.
P.O. Box 564
Hobart, IN 46342
Phone: (219) 942-1134
(Basswood)

NSI
West Hempstead, NY 11552-3942
nsitoys.com
(Be-Dazzler™ Custom hand tool, star and heart
studs)

Syndicate Sales
P.O. Box 765
Kokomo, IN 46903
(800) 428-0515
(Plastifoam® balls, Plastifoam® frames)

Therm O Web
770 Glenn Ave.
Wheeling, IL 60090
(Heat 'N Bond® Ultra Hold Iron-On Adhesive)

Wm Wright Co.
P.O. Box 398
West Warren, MA 01092-0398
www.wrights.com
(lip cord, trims, bias tape, and fringe)

Woodworkers Limited
4521 Anderson Blvd.
Fort Worth, TX 76117
(800) 722-0311
www.woodparts.biz
(2" wooden star)

Patterns

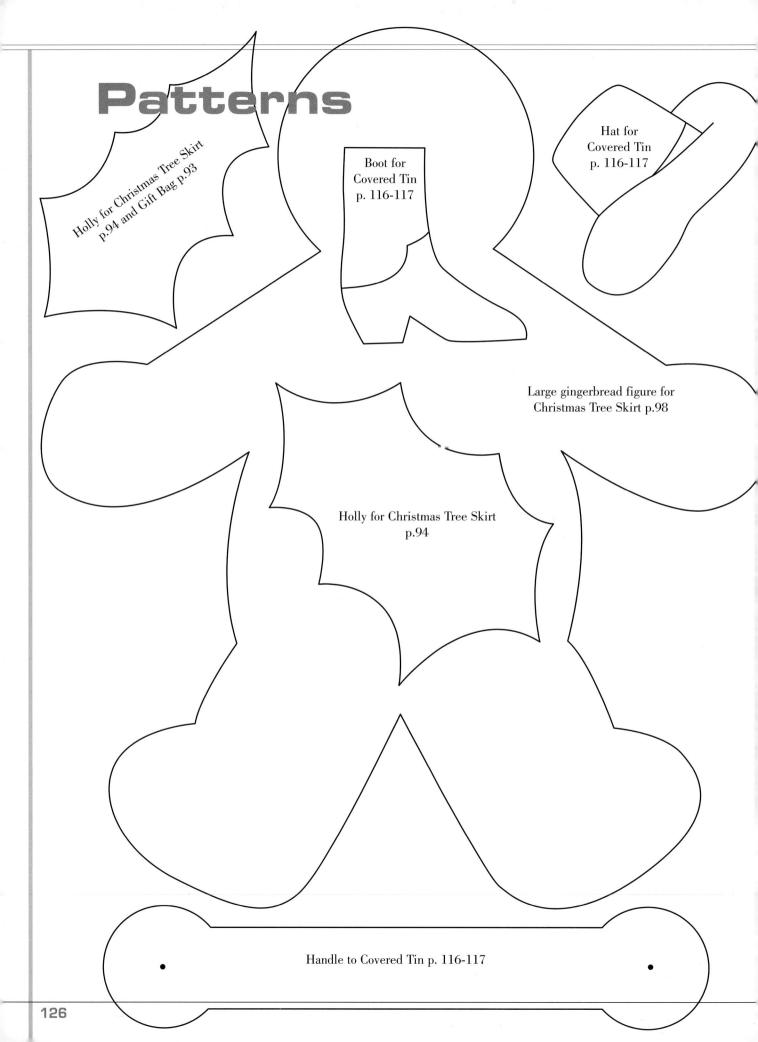

Holly for Christmas Tree Skirt p.94 and Gift Bag p.93

Boot for Covered Tin p. 116-117

Hat for Covered Tin p. 116-117

Large gingerbread figure for Christmas Tree Skirt p.98

Holly for Christmas Tree Skirt p.94

Handle to Covered Tin p. 116-117

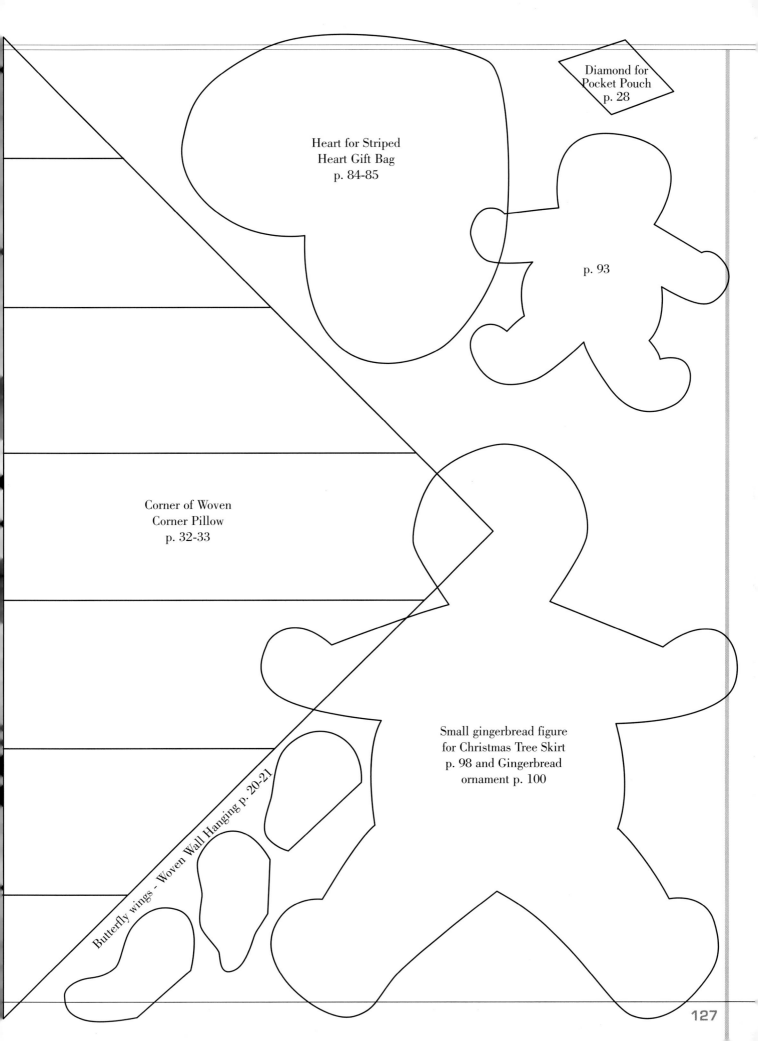

Diamond for
Pocket Pouch
p. 28

Heart for Striped
Heart Gift Bag
p. 84-85

p. 93

Corner of Woven
Corner Pillow
p. 32-33

Small gingerbread figure
for Christmas Tree Skirt
p. 98 and Gingerbread
ornament p. 100

Butterfly wings - Woven Wall Hanging p. 20-21

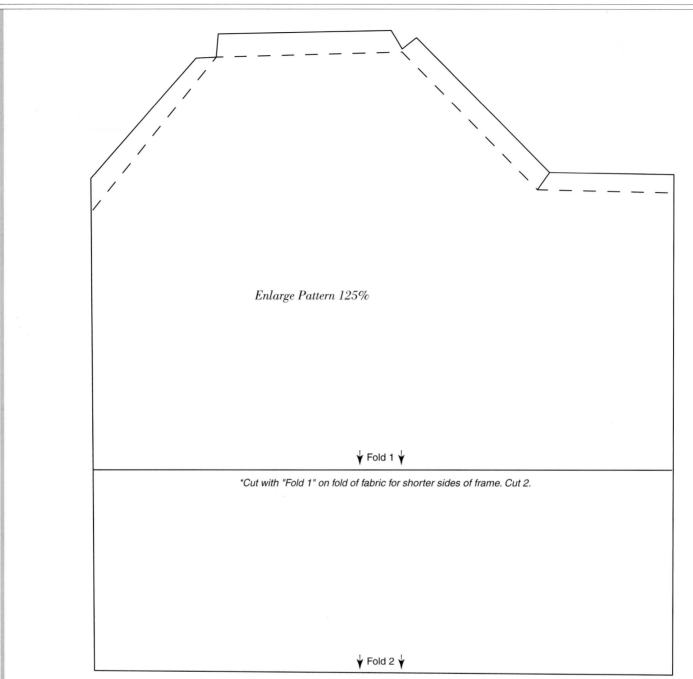

Enlarge Pattern 125%

▼ Fold 1 ▼

*Cut with "Fold 1" on fold of fabric for shorter sides of frame. Cut 2.

▼ Fold 2 ▼

*Cut with "Fold 2" on fold of fabric for longer sides of frame. Cut 2.

Pattern for Covered Frame p. 112